D1432799

# REAL LOVE, NO DRAMA

AMERICAN MUSIC SERIES

*David Menconi, Editor*

DANNY ALEXANDER

# REAL LOVE, NO DRAMA

## THE MUSIC OF
## MARY J. BLIGE

UNIVERSITY OF TEXAS PRESS ⊻ AUSTIN

Requests for permission to reproduce material from
this work should be sent to:
    Permissions
    University of Texas Press
    P.O. Box 7819
    Austin, TX 78713-7819
    http://utpress.utexas.edu/index.php/rp-form


⊗ The paper used in this book meets the minimum
requirements of ANSI/NISO Z39.48-1992 (R1997)
(Permanence of Paper).

LIBRARY OF CONGRESS CATALOGING-IN-
PUBLICATION DATA

Names: Alexander, Danny (Music journalist), author.
Title: Real love, no drama : the music of Mary J. Blige /
    Danny Alexander.
Other titles: American music series (Austin, Tex.)
Description: Austin : University of Texas Press, 2016. |
    © 2016 | Series: American music series | Includes
    bibliographical references and discography.
Identifiers: LCCN 2015035653 | ISBN 978-0-292-75943-5
    (cloth : alkaline paper)
Subjects: LCSH: Blige, Mary J. | Singers—United States—
    Biography. | LCGFT: Biographies.
Classification: LCC ML420.B649 A7 2016 |
    DDC 782.421643092—dc23
LC record available at http://lccn.loc.gov/2015035653

doi:10.7560/759435

Frontispiece by Andrew Eccles/AUGUST

*If you've been too strong for too long . . .*

# Contents

REAL
LOVE,
NO
DRAMA

*Mary speaks to the pain and struggle we as women have had and the power and strength that finding love brings, not just love of another person, but love of self. In an era when women haven't been expected to be great, Mary has done what the greats do, and that's be relevant, on a consistent basis, over a long period of time.*

Karyn White, whose three debut singles hit number one R&B the year
Mary J. Blige signed with Uptown (2013 interview with the author)

*In the urban community, Mary J. Blige preached the ghetto gospel of love and pain, triumph and change. She was the voice of a new generation of hip hop homegirls steeped in new jack and soulful melodies. She was the journal entry every woman related to, read out loud and proudly. She was the sexy, sassy, yet classy soul sista everyone wanted to be because in her they could see a lot of them, a lot of us, a lot of we.*

Portland R&B singer Toni Hill, solo artist, singer with Sirens Echo,
and member of Hungry Mob (2014 interview with the author)

*"Baggage" [a track from Mary J. Blige's 2005 album,* The Breakthrough*] represents how so many of us are holding on to the pain. . . . We understand what's weighing us down and yet we don't know how to let go. So we ask the new lover for understanding, for him/her to not give up on us. It's a universal feeling—this fear of being hurt again, a toxic emotion which depletes energy needed to sustain a new relationship. And so we keep fighting the baggage, the fear. That's all we can do. What Mary does for me, when I hear "Baggage," is validate that it's okay to be in this struggle . . . it's okay as long as you keep fighting to lighten the load, to find the courage to start over again.*

Ann Cox, mother, student, writer living in Kansas
(2014 interview with the author)

# 1

# The Artist of a Generation

The moment I began doing interviews for this book, people began giving me testimonials. Karyn White opened her interview with the above prepared statement. The server at my favorite burger joint, the editor of my school paper, my friend who cuts my hair— virtually every woman I ran into between the ages of forty-five and twenty-five (and quite a few on either side of those numbers) talked about Mary J. Blige's music with the mix of global vision and personal intimacy I've attempted to capture above. No other artist works such broad territory so closely.

Few have the consistency of output. Of the top singles artists from 1992, the year of her debut, only U2, Prince, and Mariah Carey seem particularly present in today's popular culture. Of the top-charting-album artists that year, only Bruce Springsteen, Madonna, Green Day, Bob Dylan, and Ice Cube are still well known. Only Blige, Green Day, Cube, and Carey actually emerged during this period. As one of two African American women on that list, Blige has never had the advantages and disadvantages that come with Carey's pinup beauty and five-octave vocal range.

But Blige has always had something more. Though she arrived being called a Queen of Ghetto Love and a Queen of Hip Hop

Soul, she was not celebrated for her good looks so much as her hip hop tough image. Dressing the tomboy in ball caps, jerseys, and oversized jackets, Blige conveyed the persona of a project girl with wisdom beyond her years. A hard new generation of gangsta-related rappers called her their own. Her debut album was even named *What's the 411?*, announcing her music as a key to street knowledge.

Unlike Carey's trilling vocal gymnastics, Blige's raw (sometimes flat) vocals defined the intersection of gospel and the blues. Blige sang against hard, stark beats at the height of the crack epidemic, making her a uniquely street-savvy ambassador of love and hope. Her whirlwind rise forged the reputation of her producer, Sean Combs. Her influence exploded outward as she recorded with the most eloquent gangsta, the Notorious B.I.G.; fast-talkin' jester, Busta Rhymes; the artist who defined "conscious" rap, Nas; and the coolest, most menacing member of the Wu-Tang Clan, Method Man.

That was just her first act. By her third album, she shed her producer and struck out on her own, working with some of the greatest artists in any popular music genre—Aretha Franklin, Eric Clapton, Elton John, Whitney Houston, Sting, U2, and Beyoncé. Each album a step someplace new (if not always clearly forward), she cut fourteen over the next twenty years, in addition to two remix albums and a best-of compilation. She also appeared on forty other albums as a guest artist, and she was a featured artist on over one hundred singles.

Along the way, the tomboy blossomed into a fashion-minded trendsetter and, more importantly, an icon of women's empowerment. Wearing her history of struggle, abuse, and transcendence as proudly as she came to show the scar on her left cheek that she'd long tried to hide, Mary J. Blige became something more than a diva, a queen of popular music, of popular culture, who represented the voices least represented in our society.

A quarter century after that first record, she does that job better than ever—with a voice still raw, still hip hop in its improvisational way with rhythm and possibility, but refined to such a state of control it seems there's no part of the pop music universe she can't call her own if she chooses to do so. She's recorded everything from Broadway standards to Led Zeppelin anthems, and during her 2013 duet with Michael Bublé for his Christmas TV special, the popular crooner did what so many others (from Whitney Houston to Sam Smith) have done when standing by her side—lean on her for the vision to bring the performance home.

## BEYOND DRAMA

A crucial moment in this story was her 2001 single "No More Drama." On the heels of her most successful pop single, "Family Affair," "No More Drama" was released September 22, 2001, soon after the World Trade Center was attacked. When I first saw the music video, the drumbeats of the coming thirteen years of war were audible and terrifying.

The video started by focusing on the three actors playing the central characters. They were collaged as one body, running. Blige appeared in the second scene, dressed subdued and elegant, walking the streets, a witness to tragedy. The first protagonist was a young Latino man cradling the head of a vacant-eyed friend shot down in the street. In the other scenarios, a white junkie jonesed for a fix, and a black woman suffered mental and physical abuse. Blige faced the camera and sang about choices, but she was feeling every agony playing out around her. At one point her face morphed into the bruised and swollen features of the abused woman, but Blige immediately appeared behind the woman, pulling herself from the pain of the memory by declaring, "That was long ago."

As Blige testified in a voice both racked with pain and triumphant, the addict tore a phone number and made a call for help, the young woman left her home, and the Latino youth decided not to take revenge. Each of these scenarios ended with a choice to break some kind of cycle, but the singer only grew more emphatic— her shouts and cries built in intensity, as if the real struggle had just begun.

Of course, for anyone in any form of recovery, that musical

message spoke its own truth. But the video took the analogy one step further. It ended with Blige facing a store window, a bank of TV screens flashing the news. Varied images flickered rapid-fire across those screens as if an unseen hand on a remote were desperately searching for some sign of relief. Instead, the news images bounced from police and street violence to military troops mobilizing, cities on fire, and the headline "America's New War."

At this point, the singer shook her fists and bent and shouted at the constant barrage of violence. Her voice was full of Pentecostal fire as she cried out, "Lord help me," bolstered by the rising tide of a church choir. This was the song's climax, the final full minute of music, one declaration of "no more" following after another, tying the senselessness of the street revenge to the national bloodthirst.

When I first saw that video I was shaken. This was a number fifteen pop single following up a number one pop single, and it spent twenty weeks on the pop charts. An artist known to have suffered the blows of urban neglect, street violence, addiction, and abusive relationships was making use of her personal history to diagnose a country deeply invested in denial. Today, exploring the most politically dangerous implications of what I already thought was a great record, that video still stands at an apex of my own personal history with music.

## A WHITE BOY'S RECKONING WITH
## THE VOICES OF BLACK WOMEN

My experience with "No More Drama" fulfilled a promise I grasped sometime soon after I started covering popular music for Kansas City's *Pitchweekly* and Dave Marsh's newsletter *Rock & Rap Confidential*, when I heard Salt-N-Pepa's "Push It" for the first time. That record's unhinged rhythm with its sassy, commanding female vocals sounded like nothing I'd ever heard. In fact, I wasn't sure what I was hearing, but I got it, viscerally. This was female empowerment in the guise of both a dance song and a set of instructions to fulfill a woman's needs. That record made me feel what I guess kids must have experienced hearing Little Richard or Elvis Presley for the first time—overcome by the idea of sexual liberation as the promise of rock and roll.

But much of the punk-influenced rock that greeted my adolescence shied away from straightforward love songs and could be downright prudish when it came to sex. (Even Prince's persona maintained an ironic distance.) And I understood that sensibility. As a midwestern WASP male, I was most comfortable having sexuality tackled obliquely or couched in larger social and political concerns.

As Blige would do many times on her debut, Salt-N-Pepa's "Push It" made me uncomfortable, and it was all the more thrilling for it. It stirred something sexually confrontational I loved about Joan Jett and Chrissie Hynde, but it was different. Those women rockers played a certain kind of bad girl, equal to any male's machismo, and always from a sort of undefined distance. At least to my ears, the black women aligned with hip hop closed the distance in a distinctly feminine way.

By the time Blige came on the scene, my intense identification with and attraction to black women artists had drawn me away from much interest in white boys with guitars. Of course I was working through my own racial ignorance on one level, but in a more immediate way, black women were talking about my most pressing personal issues. As a twenty-four-year-old married man, these artists hit me where I really lived.

A number one R&B hit single by Karyn White told me, "I'm not your superwoman," forcing me to think about my expectations of women, particularly the woman I had married at twenty. A number two R&B hit by Miki Howard declared that love was "under new management," hers, and I found an exhilaration in deferring to that strong feminine stance. Because marriage, particularly at a young age, can lead to a mountain of white lies, N.W.A. protégée Michel'le's number two R&B call for "No More Lies" hit home, and when En Vogue went to number one R&B with "Lies," drawing a parallel between bedroom dishonesty and that perpetuated by "the nation's leaders as well as teachers," I had to reexamine my own separation between the personal and the political.

Virtually every R&B woman had at least one such confrontation with a lover on every album, songs I came to think of as Sunday morning reckoning songs. Each of these records forced me to look at myself in the cold light of day. This was the late eighties, when hip hop was more political than ever before or since, and that spirit influenced all of R&B, so a white listener who engaged with this music was regularly invited to examine white privilege. The Sunday morning reckoning extended the self-study to family relationships. Spending hours being confronted with one's own flaws sounds a little masochistic, but more visceral and exciting things were happening at the same time. A decade later, as an antiwar statement rooted in a desire for respect at home, Blige's "No More Drama" showed the unlimited reach of the form.

But my love of a wide array of black women artists who ushered in Mary J. Blige's career actually made me a little slow to warm up to Blige herself. When Blige appeared, I was particularly taken with the Atlanta hip hop/R&B trio TLC, who had exploded onto the pop music scene a few months before with the brash, frenetic, and multilayered hip hop assault "Ain't 2 Proud 2 Beg." Blige arrived with a lot of hype other women didn't receive. She appeared to be taken more seriously by the hip hop press because producer Combs had given her a starker production style, and her voice seemed less disciplined and therefore more stereotypically "authentic" (a concept I rejected). That sound as well as the media's emphasis on her producer kept me at some distance. In retrospect, I know that means I allowed Blige to be twice victimized by her association with Combs, not giving her full credit for her work.

For my own spurious reasons then, I didn't fully embrace Blige until she dumped Combs and made 1997's *Share My World*. In the wake of TLC's *CrazySexyCool*, she'd not only made a record that followed coherently after her street-savvy aesthetic, but she'd also outdone the leading pop trio at their own game, making a slick synthesis of hip hop/R&B that rang both more unified and more mature. To my ears, this was when the hyped Queen of Hip Hop Soul began to sound majestic.

It was a difficult time, just after the murders of the two rappers who best defined a reconciliation between rap's political consciousness and its street credibility, Tupac Shakur and the Notorious B.I.G. The fact that they seemed to have both been annihilated by senseless acts of revenge was nothing short of tragic. In the wake of this violence and loss, Blige's career became a testament to survival and the enduring power of love. In that sense, she's continued to carry the torch for a generation of artists, of both genders, in R&B and rap. Almost twenty years down the line, it's hard to imagine anyone who could have done the job half so well.

## SEARCHING FOR THE SOURCE

By the summer of 2014, I'd finished a draft of this book. I felt good about what I'd written, but I knew I wasn't done. I'd planned the book knowing I might not get access to Mary J. Blige herself. Still, I wanted to challenge conventional wisdom about how contemporary R&B is made, showing the complexity of the artistic process, by talking with as many of her collaborators as I could. To reach many of those people, I needed a nod from her handlers. After over a year of being passed around and (most often) simply ignored by Blige's management, many doors remained closed to me.

I understood why. People were protective of Blige. Even I had grown protective of Blige, which made me not want to push too hard. I knew she'd had terrible press experiences at various points in her career, and 2013–2014 was a particularly controversial time in her life. The spring I began this book, she'd been hit with unpaid back taxes, and her contemporary Lauryn Hill went to jail on similar charges. Though Blige is notably always at work, this period saw her move at an unprecedented pace. While I wrote these pages, she put out three albums, acted in three different movies, and made dozens of TV appearances.

Still, one part of her untold story nagged hardest. I knew she'd spent a significant part of her childhood in Georgia, but profiles and interviews left the details very sketchy. I wanted to at least have a sense of this place and how it might have affected her, so I drove over a thousand miles to her southern childhood home. I'd tracked down a couple of relatives who were a little bit open to talking about the family history, but only a little. I made the drive because I sensed something inherently worthwhile in seeing this part of the country. I'd spent some time around Blige's other worlds in New York, New Jersey, and, later, Los Angeles, but coastal Georgia was nothing more than an abstraction to me.

It was a good thing I was prepared for the worst because it took me about three hours talking to a handful of family members to arouse the suspicions of a family matriarch. I left the family's home in Richmond Hill for Savannah worried that the few who'd talked with me would never get out of trouble with the rest of the family. (For the record, I never asked anyone specific questions about Mary J. Blige herself; that was a clear precondition in this tight-knit family.)

The next day I found myself in Savannah's Franklin Square Park on the phone with one of Blige's cousins, the Reverend Lori Blige, a minister who I had been told sings "just like Shirley Caesar." I decided to interview Reverend Blige about her own ministry, not about her famous cousin or even the family. I knew from local newspaper coverage that Reverend Blige suffered from lupus and that she was known throughout Savannah for her work helping the uninsured deal with medical issues. With a humility that seems a family trait, she downplayed these issues in our talk. Instead she chose to emphasize her plans to build a clinic focusing on the variety of issues surrounding dementia, a condition she felt went undersupported in our society. She had a soft, warm voice, but I could tell she was shy about saying too much because she, too, was concerned about where I was going with this Mary J. Blige story.

I got off the phone feeling lonesome but thankful for every little piece I'd gleaned from my conversations. Still, I'd hit a wall. I wasn't going to get more participation without causing trouble among some kind people all trying to do the right thing. The moment I accepted that dead end, my surroundings began to speak.

In the square where I sat stood a monument to the more than five hundred Haitian soldiers who'd fought alongside the colonists in the American Revolution's 1779 Battle of Savannah. The survivors went on to fight in their own 1804 Haitian Revolution against France, a slave-led rebellion opposed by the young US government. I found myself thinking about a passage I'd originally drafted as the opening to the book, Blige's performance of the 150-year-old Stephen Foster parlor song "Hard Times" for the 2010 *Hope for Haiti Now* earthquake relief telethon. Of course, Blige had recorded with members of the Haitian immigrant act the Fugees, but I'd never considered the history of interaction between blacks in the coastal South and Haitians.

The African diaspora's influence on Savannah would be made even more apparent when I took a tour of the church facing the monument, the First African Baptist Church of Savannah, established in 1777, the oldest black church in North America. The first minister of that church, Reverend George Liele, eventually fled slavery to set up another church in Jamaica.

I was there at two o'clock on a summer afternoon, and the church was filled with a couple of busloads of middle-aged and elderly black women, many in red hats. Together we learned how slaves erected the building on their own time at night in 1859. The woman tour guide told the visitors that slave women carried the materials up from the docks by torchlight, not quite joking that women's superior strength made them well suited for the task. The church ladies nodded and smiled.

We were shown Underground Railroad messages that decorated each of the original wooden pews. We descended to the basement and took a look at the crawlspaces used by the Railroad, decorative cuts in the wood based upon African designs. We were told many details of the precarious existence of this congregation throughout most of the first century of its existence, the pastors themselves having been beaten in Savannah's public squares.

Though she was born in the Bronx and moved to Yonkers, New York, by the age of ten, I knew Mary J. Blige spent much of her youth in both Savannah and Richmond Hill, just twenty miles south. All of the Bliges in America seem to come from Richmond Hill, but some family members said they have roots in South Carolina, a stone's throw in the other direction from Franklin Square.

Just standing in Franklin Square Park drove home how close Blige's roots lie to not only the heart of this country but the birth of the black church and, by extension, of American music.

That's why the Blige family roots, at least abstractly, seem important to the story of a Queen of Hip Hop Soul. After all, whether referencing Queen of Soul Aretha Franklin's records from Muscle Shoals, Alabama, or James Brown's roots in South Carolina and Georgia, talk of soul music is tied up in talk of the South, the battleground of the civil rights movement that fueled its spirit. At the same time, just as Franklin grew up in Motown and Brown rocked the Apollo in Harlem, soul music formed out of a dialogue between North and South. Hip hop had its migratory roots in Jamaican sound systems that made their way to the Bronx, where Blige was born. And rap's southern side asserted itself alongside Blige's career, hinted at by an Atlanta rap act that debuted the same year as Blige, Arrested Development.

Tidewater Georgia looks largely unchanged from old black-and-white photos of the activity surrounding Henry Ford's winter home in the town then known as Ways Station. Richmond Hill was the name of Ford's plantation, and Ford employed members of Blige's family picking okra, butter beans, and lettuce. Other photos show the tall pines Bliges cut for lumber, turpentine, and plastics when they worked for the Ford sawmill.

This is land where hard-drawn social lines blur. In the nineteenth century, rice farming Africans knew their crop better than their owners, allowing for a degree of independence that preserved the Gullah (or Geechee) culture and accent. On any given Sunday or Wednesday or Friday, Blige attended not only a distinguished red brick Baptist family church with a tall, white steeple (the family's graveyard across the street), but also the low, nondescript clapboard Holiness churches where a service's fervor could literally rock the house. In the Richmond Hill museum, the black-only and white-only classroom photos told the segregation story, but a white curator recalled good times he had running with some of the Blige brothers. Everywhere I looked, a deeper interconnectedness emerged.

The unique qualities of this place suggest something about how Blige has reached a great cross section of Americans as well as the worldwide audience to whom she's sold over fifty million albums. Blige grew up in urban poverty, but she knows the hidden, scattered poverty of the country. She knows the complexities of race relations from the concrete divisions in the city to the more subtle social distinctions that exist shoulder to shoulder in the South. Blige's roots in rural Georgia suggest a wide-angle lens that has helped her repeatedly free herself from the artistic traps that come with financial and artistic success.

Of course, that trip to Georgia only enhanced my understanding of why Mary J. Blige speaks to so many, including the Oklahoma boy writing this book. The real story lies in an enormous amount of hard work, a quick mind, and a generous heart that, despite a history of ongoing struggle, reveals itself time and time again in her music (and in connections I strive to reveal in the following pages). The more I've gotten to know this woman's dedicated personality, the more I've come to expect the self-awareness that gives her such a remarkable vision. She knows she stands for everyday women's (and men's) voices in music, just as she knows she maintains the legacy of hip hop. In other words, she knows the importance of her job, and she's serious about getting it right. For all of these reasons, I've come to see Mary J. Blige as the most important musical artist to emerge in the past quarter century.

I wanted to give Mary J. Blige the sort of book-length consideration all too rarely seen regarding black women artists or artists rooted in hip hop. Though rare compared to their white contemporaries, memoirs and biographies of such artists are not uncommon, but the kind of analysis that drew me into rock writing tends to exist only in sweeping volumes by hip hop and R&B chroniclers such as Nelson George, Jeff Chang, Tricia Rose, Brian Coleman, and Craig Werner. One of the last decade's great champions of analytic music writing about a wide variety of popular music, the single-album-centered 33⅓ Bloomsbury book series is slated to have released 122 titles by the time this book is published. One of those titles is about a black woman's work (Aretha Franklin), and three of those titles are by male hip hop artists. With this book, I want to argue against the many assumptions that tend toward the neglect of contemporary black music, its fans, and the artistry of Mary J. Blige.

Honoring all concerned, may the following pages do her justice.

# 2

# The Slow Bomb

Mary J. Blige stood in uneasy contrast to her surroundings. Her doe eyes under blonde bangs, her neck swaddled in a silver-patterned scarf, the centerpiece of her fur collar on her long, gray coat, she was an understated beauty surrounded by unadorned red brick walls in front of mud-brown painted metal doors. Her eyebrows raised as she recounted one of many occasions from her past when she saw a woman hit in the halls and on the sidewalks surrounding the Schlobohm Projects—the story she was telling having occurred right where she was standing, outside her old front door—"It looked like her head come off when he slapped her."

A woman stepped out of the brown doors, saw Blige, and put her hands on her hips in a sassy pose, grinning. Blige exclaimed, "Niecey!" And the two hugged.

"How are you?" Blige asked.

"I'm fine," Niecey said, wiping sleep from her eyes. "I woke up to come see you."

"Girl, you're on *Oprah Winfrey*." Blige laughed as Niecey—wearing a sleeveless print shirt and jeans, her hair not done—looked around a little, seemed to grow self-conscious, and quickly walked off camera. Blige laughed again, softly, both at home with her old friend and removed by the task at hand.

Inside the building, Blige walked the beige brick hallways— more like those of a high school (or maybe a prison) than a home—and mentioned the fun times she'd had in this place. But she stayed on message. The year was 2010, and Blige was on *Oprah* to promote her newly formed Foundation for the Advancement of Women Now (FFAWN), an organization based in Yonkers and dedicated to helping women get educational, career, and personal development resources. "I remember when crack first came out," she said. The epidemic took off when she was about thirteen, at that time a resident of these projects for four years. "You couldn't even come out in the hallway without smelling it. . . . And there was a lot of 'you better get upstairs' if you were by yourself because if somebody catch you in the hallway you could end up raped or something."

Ultimately, Mary J. Blige's personal story is hers to tell. She tells it best in her music, though she sometimes suggests a memoir is in the works, much further up the road. She's told the broad outlines in many interviews. She's talked of domestic abuse she witnessed, sexual abuse she suffered, drug and alcohol addiction she beat down time and time again. And she's never backed down from talking about her own abusive relationships, most famously an on-again, off-again relationship with Jodeci singer Cedric "K-Ci" Hailey throughout the 1990s. But what matters most about her story may be the contradiction she highlighted at the end of that project-visit interview.

"I could have been dead, you know, because of this environment," she said, looking around her at nothing in particular, "but because of this environment, I'm alive too." That contradiction is extraordinarily valuable if we want to seriously contemplate how the history of African American music—the blues, rhythm and blues, gospel, soul, and hip hop—comes together in this woman's art.

Of course, Mary J. Blige's music derives from wellsprings of American music far from Yonkers, and her own exposure to that music comes from many different sources. Moving back and forth between New York and Georgia, the Blige family traced and retraced the easternmost trail—straight up I-95—of the Great Migration that moved six million African Americans (alongside many poor whites) from the rural South to the urban North in the years between World War I and Blige's birth in 1971. If Blige's family had come from somewhere west of 95, they might have traveled north to Detroit, Chicago, or some other part of the industrial upper Midwest. Like an alternate version of a Motown story, it's worth noting that the demo tape that eventually broke Blige's career got passed by her mother's boyfriend to a coworker on a General Motors assembly line in New York. It's also noteworthy that Jeff Redd, the General Motors worker turned singer who passed that tape to the CEO of Uptown Records, saw the fledgling label as a new Motown. Blige's future producer, Sean Combs, told *Vibe*'s Scott Poulson-Bryant in 1993, "I wanna finish what [Motown CEO] Berry Gordy started." Blige's story reflects the larger tale of American popular music dating back the better part of a century.

In that Schlobohm segment from *Oprah*, it was apparent the place could have killed her. But everywhere Blige lived had its dangers. The day Blige was born, openly racist Lester Maddox was still governor of Georgia, and Martin Luther King Jr. had been assassinated only three years before. Though the Civil Rights Act of 1964 sought to end legalized jim crow laws six years earlier, deep divisions survived.

Blige was born into one of the most vital moments of politically charged black music. Six months prior to her birth, Motown artist Edwin Starr went to number one with his protest song "War," which he followed with another hit, "Stop the War Now." These were records that owed a great deal to the distinctly black aesthetics of James Brown's records and the emergence of the relatively new genre of music called funk, known for its loose but hard-hitting bass- and percussion-heavy groove. In that year of Blige's birth, the Temptations, Sly and the Family Stone, and James Brown himself all had strong funk singles. Aretha Franklin was breaking the Top Ten not only with covers of "Bridge Over Troubled Water" and "Spanish Harlem" but also with her own very funky "Rock Steady." When Blige was four months old, Marvin Gaye released his funky and conceptual protest record *What's Going On*.

Despite breakthroughs in the entertainment world—Flip Wilson had the first successful black variety show launching on network TV—race relations were strained throughout the country. President Richard Nixon responded to political unrest and racial militancy with his famous Southern Strategy, an appeal to working-class white America at the expense of blacks. In the spring of 1970, just up the road in Augusta, six unarmed black students were killed protesting police brutality. Days before Blige was born, black Communist Party leader Angela Davis was jailed, declaring her innocence on weapons charges. As one of its first official acts, the newly formed Congressional Black Caucus boycotted President Nixon's State of the Union address.

Almost a decade later, when Blige's father left and her mother moved her and her big sister, LaTonya, to Yonkers, New York, the Bliges walked into de facto segregation every bit as vivid as anything in the South. The Schlobohm Projects are a group of seven-story high-rises built in 1952. At that time, a boom in postwar industry, new highways (particularly the construction of the Cross Bronx Expressway), and various urban renewal efforts (often called slum clearings and at times "Negro removal") were driving upwardly mobile classes farther and farther north of Manhattan. When the "Slow Bomb" Projects were built, most of their residents were Irish and Italian immigrants.

Though redlining practices took shape in the 1920s, the years 1945 through the year of Blige's birth famously saw expanded segregationist practices that nurtured "white flight," actually building commercial development out of racial fears. Suburbs were landscaped and designed to provide relief from urban congestion, some invoking restrictive covenants to keep out the poor and minorities, while black and Hispanic neighborhoods saw rising prices and decreased access to essential services.

When nine-year-old Mary J. Blige and her family settled in Schlobohm, the Justice Department and the NAACP sued the city of Yonkers for systemic discrimination. In 1985, when Blige was fourteen, federal district court judge Leonard B. Sand handed down a six-hundred-page decision. He wrote:

> This court is fully persuaded that the extreme concentration of subsidized housing that exists in southwest Yonkers today is the result of a pattern and practice of racial discrimination by city officials, pursued in response to constituent pressures to select or support only sites that would preserve existing patterns of racial segregation, and to reject or oppose sites that would threaten existing patterns of segregation. . . . As a factual matter, the existence of such disparities has clearly worked to the disadvantage of minority students, who for many years have received their educational instruction in generally inferior facilities, from generally less experienced staff, in generally more overcrowded unstable conditions.

It is easy to see something more than family troubles led to Blige dropping out of school at the age of sixteen. She was struggling to survive the realities of a system that put a large number of black people in essentially hopeless situations.

Blige has talked frequently about the abuse, alcoholism, and drug use that surrounded her, as well as the ways she feels her education was shortchanged, leaving her ignorant of the forces manipulating her in the music industry. But, while keeping the details private, what she most often touches upon as shaping her self-image is the sexual abuse she suffered at the hands of a family friend when she was five years old. "That thing followed me all my life," she told VH1's *Behind the Music* in 2011. "The shame of thinking my molestation was my fault. It led me to believe I wasn't worth anything."

As a teenager, she grew hard. In 1995, she told *Essence's* Deborah Gregory, "[There was] always some shit going on. Every day I would be getting into fights over whatever. You always had to prove yourself to keep from getting robbed or jumped. Growing up in the projects is like being in a barrel of crabs. If you try to get out, one of the other crabs tries to pull you down." In a 2006 interview with Oprah, Blige recalled, "Before I dropped out of high school, the principal once asked me why I'd gotten in trouble. I said, 'Because I don't take no shit.' One night earlier, I'd heard my mother say that very sentence—and it was that attitude that later destroyed me. I always felt I had something to prove—because 'Mary J. Blige don't take no shit.'"

Blige recognizes there are multiple sides to her story, and she turns it over again and again. In a 2013 interview, she told Charleston's *Post and Courier*, "New York made us really street smart and tough, but the musical influence came from both the North and the South and from my grandparents." Fond memories come from singing in Baptist and Pentecostal churches in Georgia and New York as well as, at an early age, listening to her father, a jazz musician who played bass, and another uncle who played guitar. Her father had her and her sister LaTonya sing scales. At seven, Blige won a talent contest singing Aretha Franklin. Franklin was one of her mother's favorite singers, and her grounding in great women's R&B (Candi Staton, Gladys Knight, Mavis Staples, Dorothy Moore, Chaka Khan, and Patti LaBelle) as well as classic male soul (Sam Cooke, Bobby Womack, the O'Jays, and Otis Redding) seems to stem from her mother's influence. Her mother also took her to Holiness church services, where she started singing at a very young age, and Blige often cites "old gospel" as an influence on her style. She vividly recalls her father playing Roy Ayers's album *Everybody Loves the Sunshine* and associates Parliament, the Brothers Johnson, and the Isley Brothers with times spent in Georgia. Over the course of her career, she covered much of the music that was on the radio in her early childhood, including songs by the artists mentioned above as well as the Stylistics, Harold Melvin & the Blue Notes, Stevie Wonder, Rose Royce, Natalie Cole, and the Gap Band. As I rewatch that *Oprah* video, when Blige stands out back of Slow Bomb and says, "Because of this environment, I'm alive too," one thing that comes to mind is all the music that gave her strength and refuge in the fight.

As she told VH1, "Singing made me forget about all my problems and how we were living. That was my happiness." In 2011, she told the *Wall Street Journal*'s John Jurgenson that a number of people supported her in that happiness: "There was my Aunt Laura Bell. My really good friend's mother, Miss Brenda. A lady by the name of Cathy. A store up the block called Steve's Market—this was in Yonkers, on Palisades [Avenue]. I used to go there and sing for chips and grape juice. . . . I stood out, because everybody said 'Mary, sing! Mary, sing!' People wanted to hear what I could do." In 1995, on a trip with Touré back to the projects, one of her old friends told the journalist, "Anytime she was around . . . we'd all look at each other and say, 'Let's get Mary to sing.' When she finished singing, we'd all be teary-eyed."

# 3

# Ladies, Ladies, It Is Our Turn

Mary J. Blige is part of a great progression of black women's voices that have given shape to American popular music. In his groundbreaking 1963 book, *Blues People*, Amiri Baraka (then known as LeRoi Jones) declared, "The great classic blues singers were women." Baraka explained how Bessie Smith and her mentor Gertrude "Ma" Rainey, along with many others, including Ida Cox, Sara Martin, Sippie Wallace, and Bertha "Chippie" Hill, played crucial roles popularizing a more urban blues sound derived from the rural field hollers, hymns, and work songs that gave the form its birth. Of Smith, he wrote, "Her music still remained outside the mainstream of American thought, but it was much closer than any Negro music before it." Smith's 1923 recording of "Down-Hearted Blues" is said to have sold two million copies.

Baraka wrote about how the blues offered black women "an independence and importance not available in other areas open to them—the church, domestic work, or prostitution." This idea of music as a rare opportunity was echoed by the first queen of Motown, Mary Wells, in Gerri Hirshey's 1984 book, *Nowhere to Run: The Story of Soul Music*. "Until Motown, in Detroit," Wells stated, "there were three big careers for a black girl. . . . Babies, the factories or day work. Period."

In his 1971 book, *The Gospel Sound*, Anthony Heilbut discussed how women's prominence in the church—not merely as figure-heads but as the paste and mortar that held things together—laid the groundwork for their crucial role in the development of gospel music. Heilbut wrote, "The indisputable fact is that in church singing women could be peerless artists, not by denying their social situation, but by drawing upon all its elements as resources." The great gospel songwriter Thomas Dorsey was peerless as a former bluesman who modernized religious music, but the women who helped pitch his songs, Sallie and Roberta Martin, shaped the gospel circuit and defined how those songs should be performed. Sallie, in particular, came to represent a fundamental gospel value. "Her voice is all wrong," Heilbut wrote, "rough, gnarled, wide-ranging and shaky in all its registers from bass to second tenor. But 'yet and still,' Sallie Martin is the embodiment of true gospel music. . . . She is an overwhelming performer, impossible to 'outshout.'" Everyone agreed Martin knew how to make the church feel what she was feeling. Decades later, similarly qualified praise would be given to Mary J. Blige: she may not have started out with the strongest voice, but she knew how to make the audience feel what she was feeling.

Lending important insight into the history behind Blige's stance, Angela Davis's 1998 *Blues Legacies and Black Feminism* explored how Ma Rainey, Bessie Smith, and Billie Holiday responded to mainstream American ideas with distinctly black and working-class feminist values. These women celebrated individualism and sexuality as equals to their male peers. As their contemporary Zora Neale Hurston pointed out in "What White Publishers Won't Print," simply looking at (or in this case singing about) the every-day realities of black relationships challenges the assumptions of mainstream American culture, so singing about the vagaries of black women's relationships, in and of itself, has always made a social statement. But blues women also sang explicitly about social issues—from domestic abuse to prostitution to the flood of 1927 to Billie Holiday's most famous record, a record about lynching, "Strange Fruit":

*Pastoral scene of the gallant South*
*The bulging eyes and the twisted mouth*
*Scent of magnolia sweet and fresh*
*Then the sudden smell of burning flesh*

In many respects, Mary J. Blige's stardom carries forward the story of black women in every era of American music. Billie Holiday forever linked the notion of a blues singer and a jazz singer, her voice clearly an improvisational instrument of nuanced beauty. Blues singer Ethel Waters became successful on Broadway and even in Hollywood at a time when very few black women could. Queen of Jazz Ella Fitzgerald's fame accompanied the rise of the big band in the 1930s. Dinah Washington was known as the Queen of the Blues, while Mahalia Jackson (whom Heilbut called "the musical daughter of Bessie Smith") became a household name synonymous with gospel. Etta James, LaVern Baker, and Ruth Brown all had hits that prefigured rock and roll, and Brown's string of singles got the leading rhythm and blues label, Atlantic Records, dubbed "The House That Ruth Built." In the 1960s, girl groups crossed over onto the pop charts and fueled the British Invasion.

And then there was Aretha Franklin. The head of Atlantic's publicity, Bob Rolontz, told Hirshey:

> "Soul" was Aretha. What she did was something no record company could do, nobody could plan. Soul became as much of a trend as it did *because* of Aretha Franklin. Aretha came, and Aretha conquered and made that soul trend happen because it sort of united all the rest of the artists behind her. She hauled them in a mighty wake.

Blige gets referred to as a queen of "soul" because of those associations with Franklin and with a very specific era in black music tied to a rising black consciousness. As Nelson George wrote in 2004's *Post-Soul Nation*: "As the sixties progressed, soul signaled not simply a style of pop music but the entire heritage and culture of blacks. . . . We became 'soul sistas' and 'soul brothers' who dined on 'soul food', exchanged 'soul shakes', celebrated with 'soul claps' as 'soul children' marching for 'soul power' while listening to 'soul brother number one', James Brown." George continues to discuss how quickly the term "soul" descended into branding for the sale of commodities, but the essential concept survives as a stamp of quality for secular black art with deep roots in the black church, the cornerstone of the black community.

Blige has often drawn upon those black women's voices that fueled the soul music of her early childhood and even the far more co-opted disco movement that followed on its heels, covering Dorothy Moore, Chaka Kahn, Gwen Dickey (of Rose Royce), Natalie Cole, and, of course, Aretha Franklin. As Blige later did, most of these women—along with Gladys Knight, the Pointer Sisters, Ann Peebles, and Donna Summer—bridged audiences as cultural differences increased.

The significance of Blige's hip hop influence comes out of the next chapter of the pop music story. By the late seventies, FM rock stations waged "Disco Sucks" campaigns, burning disco records in stadiums. The punk rock movement that emerged in 1977 was predominately white and male, but strong women rockers such as Deborah Harry, Patti Smith, Chrissie Hynde, the Go-Go's, and Joan Jett challenged those gender norms. Born in more or less the same moment, the black do-it-yourself underground dubbed "hip hop" inspired both genders to participate in its music, dance, and art revolution.

The black women whose voices directly prefigure Blige took firm hold of the pop charts by the mid-eighties. In some ways, Tina Turner's greatest successes in her forties signaled a new kind of woman unprecedented in the pop charts—sexually worldly, independent, and demanding "You better be good to me." Her hit singles overlapped with those of newcomer Whitney Houston, who had seven number one hit crossovers in 1985 and 1986. And, in 1986, Janet Jackson launched her own string of six Top Ten crossover hits, important for at least two primary reasons. Jackson's second hit single from her album *Control*, "Nasty," with its huge percussive swing, would later be cited as the birthplace of the new jack R&B movement of the late eighties, the original attempt to forge a fusion between hip hop and R&B. Just as important, though, was the album title track. No doubt inspired at least in part by Madonna's self-assertive presence at the top of the charts, Jackson focused this slinky jam on one goal—"I don't want to rule the world, just want to run my life."

Despite their success on the charts, women before the hip hop era were rarely thought of independently from their producers or other males who managed their careers. The girl groups were most associated with Berry Gordy at Motown and Phil Spector at Philles. The breakthrough years of Aretha Franklin's career are greatly associated with producer Jerry Wexler and famously marked by a volatile relationship with husband Ted White. Tina Turner's famous divorce from rock and soul pioneer Ike Turner, and subsequent accounts of domestic abuse, helped to highlight the often oppressive environment women faced in the music industry.

Women who attempted to gain control of their careers often paid a steep price for standing up for their rights. In her 1996 autobiography, *Miss Rhythm* (written with Andrew Yule), Ruth Brown recalled how she eventually couldn't get past the lobby of the record company she helped build. Martha Reeves, of Martha and the Vandellas, told Hirshey, "I think I was the first person at Motown to ask where the money was going . . . and that made me an enemy. Did I find out? Honey, I found my way out the door."

Asked how difficult the music business was for women in the late eighties, a key player in the crafting of hip hop soul and a direct influence on Blige, Miki Howard, said (in a 2013 interview with the author),

First, you have to separate that out to talk about white women and African American women in the industry. Madonna and Celine Dion have certain advantages, you know, that black women do not have. One is the support system, and one is the ability to go straight to the pop charts. If you were black, you weren't able to just walk in those doors like that. It's like today, people are going crazy over the issue of the N-word, you can't say *nigger*, well, how would you like to be a *nigger* and a *bitch*? So, that's what you were facing as an African American woman in show business. You were a nigger bitch!

In terms Blige came to understand all too well, all too soon, Howard broke down the modest needs that could bring on the slur:

I used to stretch myself to do anything I could, but the efforts were futile. People still call you a bitch. They still don't accommodate your needs. And you're still way too tired to sing. And when it seems like that starts to happen, then you have to put your foot down. No, I'm not going to the meet and greet, I can't make it, I have to go to bed. No, I'm not flying in early in the morning and then performing at seven o'clock. You know, stuff like that, and then they say, you're a bitch.

"Whatever," she said, laughing, "I'm going to be a well-rested one." She laughed again. "So I can do my job."

---

Blige's career caught merging waves of women in rap and R&B who were challenging such barriers. In the wake of Janet Jackson's 1986 hit with *Control*, sweet-voiced R&B singers with a similarly funky call for independence began to storm the charts, most notably Jody Watley in 1987, with fierce, sophisticated singles about romantic independence, and Pebbles in 1988, whose two biggest hits, "Girlfriend" and "Mercedes Boy," made distinctly important political statements. "Girlfriend" was a sister-to-sister call to not let any man "treat you so bad," and "Mercedes Boy" served well as a rejoinder to Prince's "Little Red Corvette," the woman embracing an even finer car as a metaphor for her sexuality, proud of both her economic and sexual power.

Although the early years of recorded hip hop were dominated by male voices, women rappers became a significant force in the industry during the mid-1980s. As Tricia Rose pointed out in her

1994 book *Black Noise*, Salt-N-Pepa's 1986 platinum debut sold almost as well as Run-D.M.C's mainstream breakthrough. And the meaning of the women rappers' success was not lost on the artists or their audience. Cheryl James (a.k.a. Salt) told Rose: "The women look up to us, they take us dead seriously. It's not a fan type of thing; it's more like a movement."

The women of hip hop, often referred to as B-girls, had been around since the form first took shape out of block parties in the Bronx and other urban neighborhoods that lay claim to pieces of this story. If it was Kool Herc's great Jamaican sound system that made him stand out in the Bronx, Jamaican immigrants, male and female, also shaped the beach hip hop culture that came into being in places like Miami. In particular, though, the New York boroughs and the Southside of Philly seemed to be the origin points—places where young men and women, mostly black and Hispanic, responded to deindustrialization, urban neglect, and unemployment with cultural celebrations that included explosions of brightly colored art on any surface available, acrobatic new dance moves to fit on a scrap of old cardboard, and new music forged out of the best bits of old records. A new breed of deejays came to life in the era of the mobile disco party. The mobile disco unit allowed a deejay to set up anywhere and play a continuous set of dance hits, fading from one turntable to the next in an endless medley of beats.

Now, rapping, or stylized talking, had been a part of African American culture about as long as Africans had been forced to adopt English, but the tradition took on new forms in the South Bronx and other hotbeds of the emerging form. The South Bronx's DJ Hollywood is most often credited with being the first to start creating a different kind of musical montage with such beats. He'd focus on the most exciting moments on a record, an instrumental, especially percussive, break, and play it over and over. He'd play two of the same records at the same time, throwing bits of one copy against pieces of the other. And he'd rap to his dancers over the mix. Certain things DJ Hollywood said at his parties, like "Now put your hands in the air, and wave 'em like you just don't care," became a part of hip hop tradition. That said, it wasn't long before the MC, or rapper, became a separate musical participant, dazzling the crowd on a par with the break-dancers. When three of those rappers were pulled together for 1979's "Rapper's Delight," hip hop became a national phenomenon with men at the center (though the producer behind that first single was a woman, Sylvia Robinson, famous two decades before for her role in "Love is Strange" duo Mickey & Sylvia).

The vast new polyrhythmic possibilities pioneered by hip hop deejays like Afrika Bambaataa producer Arthur Baker, Run-D.M.C.'s Jam Master Jay, and Grandmaster Flash influenced all of eighties popular dance music and moved it away from the rote patterns of seventies disco. With all of the beats more complex and swinging harder than before, eighties R&B seemed to be searching for a way to connect with the hip hop movement. Very often, for the reasons stated above, this took the form of male producers trying to give a hip hop context to the work of female R&B performers. Jimmy Jam and Terry Lewis were the producers behind those Janet Jackson records, while Prince associate André Cymone used a similar approach with Jody Watley. Producers Foster and McElroy seemed to want to synthesize every black musical style since big band with the quartet En Vogue. And another duo, from the R&B group The Deele, L.A. Reid and Kenneth "Babyface" Edmonds, were the force behind Pebbles's hits. While producer Teddy Riley famously gave this sound the name new jack swing to promote his 1988 Keith Sweat album (and then his own group, Guy), L. A. Reid and Babyface consistently focused the same musical ideas on new ways to showcase women.

---

Just as Blige's producer Sean Combs would, for a time, get credit for Blige's work, the role of male producer typically became exalted over that of female performer—no matter who might actually be driving the changing sounds in the studio. In a 2013 interview with the author, Dorothy Moore, a star whose 1975 version of "Misty Blue" Blige heard as a child and eventually covered (in

1998) around the same time as teenage R&B singer Monica, made it very clear her hit was a matter of collaboration, with producers Tommy Couch and James Stroud deferring to her judgment.

The original record is famously a one take, rooted in Moore's reinterpretation of a song by her friend Nashville songwriter Bob Montgomery. Based in Jackson, Mississippi, Moore would stop in Nashville when the road took her there and hear the best new material by the best writers. Now, "Misty Blue" had already been a Top Ten country hit for both Wilma Burgess and Eddy Arnold, but Moore had her own ideas about how it might work.

She recalled,

At the beginning of it is a hum, and that was my creation. I thought of it. What happened was, the intro, when they got ready to release it, I told them to wait before they would do that because I had an idea. I'd had a copy for two years listening to it, and I knew it back and forth. So I went into the studio, and they let me come in and record that. I didn't want to tell them what I wanted to do. I told them, "Just turn the machine on and everything, and let me record what I want to do," and I'd let them know when I thought I had finished. I put a little cut [hand gesture] under my throat to let them know I was finished. But it was that hum. The intro was so long with nothing but music, they didn't have anything there. So that's what I did.

She adds, "They usually accepted everything that I did. They used to ask me was I satisfied."

Despite the similar power most great women singers must have asserted in the studio, that story has rarely been told. Only in gospel and early urban (what Amiri Baraka calls "classic") blues have women received anything approaching equal attention, and that attention is generally confined to discussions of Bessie Smith and Billie Holiday. While music has always been a form in which women could shine, particularly as singers, the privileging of male achievement over that of women affected the way people used the music. Young women were the ones famously screaming and swooning in large numbers when Frank Sinatra or Elvis or the Beatles performed, while young men wanted to be those stars. Female artists almost never gained both audiences. Boys have typically not listed the music made by women as "their music."

The girl group era of the early 1960s broke some new ground. Young men not only crushed on Mary Weiss of the Shangri-Las or Ronnie Spector of the Ronettes, but they were likely to see those women as part of the gang. In the 1970s, the tough sounds of punk rockers like Patti Smith, Chrissie Hynde, and Joan Jett made them frontline stars who could go toe to toe with their male counterparts.

Similar to those punk rockers, the first commercially successful female rap MCs—Salt-N-Pepa, MC Lyte, Queen Latifah, Roxanne Shanté, and the Real Roxanne—were up against a form that was identified, like hard rock and punk, as fundamentally masculine. In many ways, post-seventies (which generally meant post-soul and, in some sense, post-black-consciousness) R&B had gathered some of the stigma associated with disco. Male hip hoppers were likely to see mainstream R&B as a slick commercial product, and some dismissed popular rhythm and blues by calling it "romance and bullshit." To the extent that hip hop rebelled against mainstream music, it bucked against R&B itself. The fact that R&B featured many female acts and was more associated with women audiences reinforced the masculine character of the rebellion.

Still, some maintained distance from the untenable nature of that contradiction and sought a way to at least reconcile the genders. Hip hop producers like Marley Marl and Hurby "Luv Bug" Azor backed Roxanne Shanté and Salt-N-Pepa, while rap crews developed female talent. N.W.A. worked with Michel'le, Ice Cube with Yo-Yo, and Public Enemy with Sister Souljah. Israeli singer Ofra Haza's sample on a remix of Eric B. & Rakim's 1987 hit "Paid in Full" brought new dimensions to the duo's austere MC and turntable approach, and before long they cut a single with Jody Watley. No doubt because it was in their interest to find the tenor of the times, R&B producers pushed hardest to break down the barriers between the two forms.

"I worked with the most sought-after producers," Karyn White recalled. Her first single, 1988's "The Way You Love Me" was an L. A. Reid and Babyface cut that gave a frenetic new femininity to the fusion now called new jack swing. "It started with Jam and Lewis, especially with Janet and 'Control.' That whole marriage opened up the way for Babyface and L. A., and I felt blessed because everybody wanted their production."

If there is a single record that anticipates Blige's famous refrain "too strong for too long," it would probably be White's second single, "Superwoman," a confrontation between a man and a woman about her need for limits. But that record was an R&B song that didn't show obvious signs of hip hop. In the flux of that musical era, this L. A. Reid and Babyface record reached to a wellspring of musical vitality parallel to but separate from hip hop: the music of Prince, an influence on all of these producers. White affirmed this connection. "On stage we go through this whole 'Purple Rain' solo with my guitar player," she said of her performances of "Superwoman," "and sing the 'Ooh, ooh, ooh, ooh' [echoing the Prince track]."

Of her 1988 debut, White singled out the feature that most clearly distinguishes her and connects her work to Blige: "After working on six or seven up-tempo numbers, Face wrote 'Superwoman' for me. When they played it for me, I was like 'wow,' it was just so beautiful. It was this sad but powerful story. I remember being in awe. So, I'm glad they saw me as the type of artist who could sing that song. That's what a great producer does. They know how to match the right song with the right artist."

From the vision of the song to the tenor of the vocal, the aesthetic L. A. Reid and Babyface chased with White anticipated the qualities that would set Mary J. Blige apart. White recalled, "When we recorded 'Superwoman,' we sang that over and over and over. They probably made no money from the production because we were trying so hard to find the magic. L. A. and Face liked the raw—I don't care if it's a little off-key—emotion, give it to me gutsy. I can relate to Mary in that she sang that way too. It wasn't perfect; it was true." And then, as an aside, White added, "Of course, today, Mary's got that raw emotion, and she's *on point*."

Though White expressed no animosity toward her producers, producers much beloved by a long list of women artists, even L. A. Reid and Babyface's relationship with women in the studio suggests volumes about the imbalance of power between men and women in the industry. White recounted, "L. A. would stay and work with me on the vocals, making me upset and calling me all kind of names when we were recording 'Superwoman.' I didn't know who that woman was. I hadn't lived life for real yet. I had to draw from my mother. I was too young. But I was glad that they saw me like that because that song separated me from the Janet Jacksons and the Pebbleses because it was an anthem for women."

White's account of that era, working with both L. A. Reid and Babyface as well as Jimmy Jam and Terry Lewis, and its relationship to Mary J. Blige's significance, lays important groundwork. What Reid and Babyface were pushing for, that woman's voice, was a depth of emotion and maturity that could not be denied, what once gave "soul" music a weight all but lost in the crossover eighties. Babyface would later work with Blige on the single "Not Gon' Cry" to push her to a similarly new level of sophistication. Meanwhile, in 1988, the greatness of "Superwoman" lay outside the bounds of hip hop.

---

In 1989, the rap label Def Jam took a more radical approach to finding a new synthesis with their remarkable backup singer Alyson Williams. Williams had worked with R&B stars Melba Moore and Meli'sa Morgan before joining Def Jam and shining as a duet partner with their male vocalists Chuck Stanley and Oran "Juice" Jones. Her debut album was called Raw, and it followed the typical R&B style of up-tempo on the A-side and a slow jam (a.k.a. "quiet storm") B-side. The difference in this case was that Williams's A-side was clearly a hip hop production.

In a 2013 interview with the author, Williams explained,

What Russell [Def Jam label head Russell Simmons] did, his vision was, he put together the most hip hop beats I could do and then put smooth vocals over the top of them. That's what the attempt was, and that's what they did. We took a good track like "My Love is Raw" and "Sweet Talk" and we sang on top of it. And then we did a classic thing like "Just Call My Name," you know? There was a pattern that Blige was able to follow after that. So, whatever her title is of Queen of Hip Hop Soul, there's an Original Queen of Hip Hop R&B.

Williams's solo debut was the first album-length effort to declare a new form equal parts hip hop and R&B. But it was the classic R&B, the ballad "Just Call My Name," that was most commercially successful. Williams remained an R&B figure connected to hip hop but somehow not of it. Blige, by contrast, would emerge as a voice for hip hop itself.

# 4

# Uptown

The first glimpse most pop fans had of Mary J. Blige was as a backup singer for Father MC, in his video "I'll Do 4 U." By no means a classic, the video still revealed the power women could have, even as secondary players, in an evolving hip hop scene. A little over a year into the sensation caused by MC Hammer's acrobatic stage presence, Father MC and two footloose wingmen danced their rears off, pledging to everyone else in the video—the screaming women in the audience, the remote women in his backing band (traces of Robert Palmer's "Addicted to Love," but less creepy), and his backup singers, all dressed in black and making fairly simple gestures to the beat. Everything about this video reinforced the idea that men have to earn women's attention and respect.

Of the backup singers, it was the seemingly small blonde up front who stood out. She didn't necessarily call attention to herself, but she looked different—young and innocent with big eyes and a pixie cut. At first, she bided time, swinging her arms to the rhythm, but then she sang, growling responses to the MC, and she soon became the strongest personality onstage. Somehow, she seemed a part of the act and separate at the same time, like some big fan got a turn at the mic, and now she was showing everyone else the real possibilities in the song.

In some ways, that's how it was. Though signed to Uptown Records for almost three years already, Mary J. Blige was still just a teenager. Her life was about to change dramatically, but, at this point, it was still that of the Yonkers project girl who made some money doing her friends' hair and working as a phone directory assistant.

Still, her story was moving fast. At seventeen, Blige couldn't have known her mall recording of an Anita Baker hit, "Caught Up in the Rapture," was going to take her anywhere. Baker's record is a very adult record, a sophisticated, sensual reverie. Blige did something different with it—described again and again as racked with pain—that made people take notice.

On that 2011 *Behind the Music*, Blige said, "Everybody loved it," including her mother's boyfriend, Jimmy Dillard. Dillard, a worker at a GM plant in Tarrytown, New York, surprised Blige with his response. "He loved it," she added, smiling. "He was all happy about it, and he was like, I know somebody that can help you!"

She laughed at the memory. "And I'm looking at him like, 'Who do you know that can help?'" She laughed again.

But Jimmy Dillard did know someone. He knew a young singer named Jeff Redd who had just signed with Uptown Records. Uptown had been founded by former Dr. Jeckyll & Mr. Hyde rapper Andre Harrell, a man who had worked with the leading rap label, Def Jam (Run-D.M.C., Beastie Boys, LL Cool J), on its Rush Associated Labels. One-time Harrell colleague and author of 2011's *The Tanning of America: How Hip-Hop Created a Culture That Rewrote the Rules of the New Economy*, music producer Steve Stoute gave Harrell a great deal of credit for tilling the ground where a true fusion of hip hop and soul might flourish.

"Andre saw in the late eighties," Stoute wrote, "how the hard-edged drama of rap music, with the thumping drums and bass-heavy groove that were the signature of Def Jam artists, was not incorporating all the rich cool smoothness and bright musicality that had built the house of R&B. The question he asked was, how can we make this less rough around the edges, give it more soul and R&B, put guys in suits and add glamour."

Jeff Redd certainly was the right guy for such a suit. Redd's smooth vocals on "Love High" and "What Goes Around, Comes Around" managed to soar and dance all over a beat. Good-looking and a fine dancer himself, Redd defined Uptown Records with all the sophistication of labelmates Guy, as well as a healthy dose of the warmth and playfulness of the label's other leading male act, Heavy D & the Boyz.

When I talked with him in 2013, Jeff Redd described that era when things were changing so fast that every closed door felt like a new opportunity. Redd recalled,

> I got my deal in 1988. And Blige got signed in 1989. Little Jimmy [Dillard] and I worked together at General Motors on the assembly line, so he would see flyers and posters of me performing here and there. That's what I was doing with the money I was making at General Motors, making flyers and doing shows, paying bands, getting clothes made. I got my deal because Andre Harrell saw me perform at a show, and afterwards, he came backstage and said, "Welcome to the Uptown family."
>
> Because I didn't finish my deal until November 1988, and I never stopped working at General Motors, that's where I found Mary J. Blige. Little Jimmy said, "I heard you got on," and said, "Maybe you could do a thing with my daughter." He gave me a cassette. And she was singing. . . . I can't remember which Anita Baker it was, possibly "Caught Up in the Rapture." So I heard it and I said, "You know, she's pretty good." I could hear the sound of the pain in her voice; she must have had a struggle going on within her.

"Everything was happy at that time, when new jack came along, until Mary's generation came around," Redd said. After over a decade of economic downturn in the inner city, along with the rise of crack cocaine and the death toll of youth caught up in the violence surrounding this inexpensive and highly addictive drug, hip hop was turning darker by the late eighties. The militant sounds of Public Enemy and the gangsta threat of Compton's N.W.A. were defining the cutting edge of rap. "By the grace of God, I was able to see what was coming next," Redd observed on Blige's *Behind the Music.* "I heard a lot of pain and a lot of joy at the same time, which was, and still is, the voice of young America."

So Redd took the tape to Harrell. "When I heard her voice," Harrell told VH1, "it was so beyond anything else I'd ever experienced or had the opportunity to work with. It wasn't even a thought about signing her. I couldn't wait to sign her."

But over four years passed between Blige's initial deal and the release of her first album. Redd recalled in our interview, "She was only seventeen at the time, and I remember her mother had to sign her deal. The following year, when she turned eighteen, she was able to sign her own deal."

"We were very close," Redd continued, "and we all grew a little disillusioned about the record business. I know I thought my record would be out by summer '88, not knowing it would be two and a half years before it came out. And it was the same situation with her. She got a deal in '89, but with the little advance she had, everybody went through their money, and I remember her calling my house and saying, 'Where are you, I need to get something to eat.'" Redd would come get her and take care of her as best he could.

Fortunately, that period was also a time of excitement. "Uptown Records was located in Brooklyn," Redd went on, "and I remember one day Andre and I went upstairs, and these four guys were singing. And we said, 'Who are you guys?' They said, 'Yo, I'm JoJo, and this is K-Ci, and he's my brother,' and another one says, 'And I'm DeVante, and this is Dalvin, my brother. . . . We drove from North Carolina.'

"And we said, 'You're going to be signed to Uptown Records.'" Those musicians who drove up north and auditioned in the office were Jodeci, an act that went on to have eleven hit singles and would subsequently spin off K-Ci & JoJo, who would later go on to have their own successful singles.

At that time, Redd said,

We did not know that our passion for making music would lead us to such great success. We were just doing what we loved. A lot of the music that we made was recorded in various locations and would sometimes be made within someone's home.

The great thing about Uptown was that everyone did many things. Everyone contributed in various ways. We all took a part in it. If you had told us that we were making records that would still be relevant today, we wouldn't have believed it. We were making records that were good for us, that would sound good in the streets, that deejays would play. That was a great time for music. The album had to take form and take shape. The artists had to be developed. I had to go all around the country and do interviews, and open up for this person and that person.

I had Mary doing background on my album, and I would have her perform as well. We did the Apollo together, and she sang background with me. And then when she finished that record "You Remind Me" for the *Strictly Business* soundtrack, I would have her perform it in the middle of my set.

That soundtrack cut was Blige's first solo record, and Redd remembered it didn't come easy. "I was there when Mary made 'You Remind Me' with [Uptown producer] Dave Hall. And she was just trying to figure it out and get it going. He was doing a lot of the writing, and he was just trying to get her to get some notes and get on it. This was before Auto-Tune and all that stuff. They had a thing called Pitch Time or something like that, but you still had to be on the note. I'll never forget her singing that song for about three days trying to hit the note."

But a young intern serving as talent director at the label knew Blige was worth every minute he could give her. He got her project off the ground, feeling strongly that Blige had what was missing in R&B and initially dubbing her the "Queen of Ghetto Love." His decision to produce her album would make a star of Sean Combs.

*My top 5 MJB songs/features are: "I Love You," "Real Love," "You're All I Need to Get By," "What's the 411?" and "Be without You." There's so many more, but those stay with me in regular rotation. No one in hip hop has outlasted Mary J. Blige. She's talented, relevant, versatile, indispensable, and truly amazing.*

Mia Styles, deejay/music producer at B-Girl Media
(2014 interview with the author)

# 5

# What's the 411?

Released on July 28, 1992, Mary J. Blige's debut album, *What's the 411?*, arrived at a time of great cultural upheaval in America. That spring, following the acquittal of four police officers who brutally beat motorist Rodney King, South Central Los Angeles exploded into rioting. Rioting also occurred in other cities—most notably Tampa and West Las Vegas. The L.A. riots lasted from April 29 through May 3, when 3,500 US troops joined the California National Guard and quelled the rebellion. At the end of it all, sixty-three people would be dead, at least ten killed by police, and two thousand injured.

Rather than acknowledge the way rappers illuminated real causes for the riots—including at least four decades of documented LAPD racism, two decades of South Central deindustrialization, and a five-year spike in youth violence caused by the advent of crack cocaine, presidential candidate Bill Clinton famously used the moment to focus attention on the perceived dangers of rap music and rap music's ideology, comparing black nationalist rapper Sister Souljah to former Ku Klux Klan Grand Wizard David Duke. Lines were being drawn. Rapper Ice-T put out his heavy metal record "Cop Killer," and a similar fantasy, the single "Deep

Cover" by Dr. Dre and relative unknown Snoop Dogg, set the stage for the G-funk phenomenon *The Chronic* later that year. The first popular southern rap crew, Arrested Development, topped the charts that summer with "Tennessee," an alienated meditation on the lynching of black Americans.

As always, the pop charts soothed pain as much as or more than they expressed anger. The day the riots started, a ballad by Atlanta's contenders for queens of hip hop R&B, TLC, began to climb the charts with a strong women's anthem declaring love on a woman's terms, "Baby-Baby-Baby," the latest in a series of such songs written and produced by Babyface. In June, Philadelphia soul quartet Boyz II Men released another Babyface song, "End of the Road," which became the biggest single of that year. The gospel-tinged love song broke a record by Elvis Presley, staying at *Billboard*'s number one slot for thirteen weeks (a record that would be topped immediately by Whitney Houston's cover of Dolly Parton's "I Will Always Love You").

In the earliest stories about Blige's debut record, she was already getting called the "Queen of Hip Hop Soul." *What's the 411?* offered a rough-edged, tender-hearted search for hope, and her job title demanded a social consciousness that spoke to the anger in hip hop. Though her former job as a phone operator helped name the album, "411" was hip hop slang for street knowledge. In this case, the 411 was that Mary J. Blige had arrived, and what she offered was the hope that comes from self-worth, truth, love, and commitment—all the things she was searching for and all the things she symbolized from day one.

---

You could hear this multilayered message from the moment that record hit the street, and that meaning remains vivid today. Its very first sounds—a rhythmic, mechanical intake and exhale of air, a drum sample, and a squeak of keyboard—announce this is, indeed, a hip hop record. Those sounds loop while the not-yet-famous "Puff" frets and rants at a ringing telephone. When he gets a chance to leave a message, he's apparently frustrated with his rough-hewn, would-be star—"Yo, I know you're there, man. . . . Pick up!" There's an ongoing argument between producer and artist just beneath the surface, and the sound of the record seems a nod to 1989's "No More Lies," also an argument between another hip hop singer, Michel'le, and her gangsta producer, N.W.A.'s Dr. Dre. While people tend to think of hip hop intros as superfluous nods to an obligatory tradition, this one establishes street cred and hints at how much producer Combs styled his tough yet danceable approach to hip hop on the sounds coming from South Central Los Angeles's gangsta rappers.

But that's only the first forty seconds of a cut that continues for three more minutes. Twelve messages follow—major players responding to the hype, wanting Blige's ear. The innovative rapper who proved slow talking could have every bit the force of rapid-fire rhymes, EPMD's Erick Sermon, calls to wish Blige luck. Cold Chillin's star Kool DJ Red Alert tries to warn her she's making a mistake not working with him. Jeff Redd's new rival at Uptown Christopher Williams wants a duet. Heavyweight rapper C. L. Smooth wants her for a remix. Journalist Jamie Brown of *Sister 2 Sister* wants an interview. Heavy D just wants to party.

Though she does not get a writing or production credit on this record, and she would never claim the vision of this record as her own, this is how the world met Mary J. Blige. Blige arrived with a reputation that she would speak authoritatively, as an artist with a vision. What's surprising about *What's the 411?* is just how fully formed Blige's voice already seems. Sean Combs may have had an uncanny sense of what his friend offered as an artist, but Blige herself seems to know how to project her vision through these vehicles. Whatever the explanation, this debut serves as a solid foundation for all that came after.

Blige begins with a sweetly voiced love song, "Reminisce," a call to rekindle lost romance. The record's burbling bass always seems to be building, trying to get something going, but then it collapses, notes descending rapidly, before finding its way forward again. Male backing vocalists call to "reminisce on the love we had," urging the couple in the song to give it another try. The spare arrangement—generally just keys, those vocals, and that bass line—as well as Blige's straining, free-form lead, all say hip hop.

That said, the song also starts with a soulful element, strings suggesting a classic pop ballad behind Blige's jazzy vamps. And soul, coming as it does from the black church, always hints at a message for the community. From these beginning moments, this focus on community is one of the things that kept Blige in a dialectic with the increasingly individualistic norms of hip hop. Blige's approach chases what author Craig Werner calls the "gospel impulse" (in his 1999 *A Change Is Gonna Come*, building on the ideas of Ralph Ellison regarding black aesthetics, particularly the more individually transcendent blues impulse and the more innovation-focused jazz impulse). The gospel impulse is a philosophy and a process by which artists (particularly soul musicians, most directly influenced by the gospel tradition) move beyond individual strength to build community and hope out of life's inevitable struggle. Blige uses all of these impulses in her work, but the secular use of the gospel impulse is what she most distinctly develops at the heart of American popular music.

In 1992 America, the way Blige lingers on "I can remember when we had, we had love . . . you and I, you and I," listeners couldn't help but yearn for a lost innocence. "Make some time tonight," Blige urges, trying to carve out time and space to remember what it felt like to enjoy each other. On some level, it's the primary goal of making music, but it's not a state of mind Blige can take for granted.

What follows are Blige's first two number one R&B hits, "You Remind Me" charting number twenty-nine and "Real Love" charting number seven on the Top Forty, crossing over to the pop charts higher than her next eleven singles. It seems no coincidence that this song, Blige's second single, bears the same name as a Jody Watley R&B number one (Top Forty no. 2) from three summers before. The song anchored her in a direct line of tradition. Jody Watley's "Real Love" exemplifies the empowered-women records that followed Janet Jackson's new jack prototype—a woman striking out on her own over blasts of keyboard and a wall of percussive sound.

Blige's record has some overt similarities—most notably its upbeat rhythm and refrain, both recalling and summarizing Watley's hit. But the differences are vast. Blige's songwriters (Mark C. Rooney and Mark Morales) tell the entire story of a relationship with that refrain. First, she's asking a lover to give her what she needs. After he fails her time and again, she prays that her disappointments won't keep her from striving for what she deserves. When she finally makes the break, she begins vamping on the title phrase, her voice behind the backup singers. Down low in the mix, she whoops and hollers and even growls, looking for the strength she finds by the end, her voice high and loud and strong as she testifies that she's searched all around the world and come to the conclusion there is no one who will set her heart free.

Despite the heartache, this record sounds liberated. The bubbling bass and keys practically skip their way forward, and there's a playfulness between Blige and the backup singers that almost sounds like kids at recess (occasionally featuring breaks that sound like cheers for a B-boy or B-girl breaking). In the turbulent racial climate of 1992, this number seven crossover hit revels in the blackness of its sound, setting Blige's debut apart from most of the pop music that sprung from Janet Jackson's success. No doubt that's why, even though the *New York Times* handed her the "new jill swing" moniker almost immediately after her record's release, four months later, James T. Jones IV wrote in *USA Today*, "She prefers the term hip-hop soul over new jack swing. 'There's a difference. It's more street.'"

The following song, "You Remind Me," was actually Blige's debut single, released almost a year earlier as a part of the *Strictly Business* soundtrack and then rereleased a month before *What's the 411?* Here, it's a hip-pocket summation of all that's come before— "You remind me of a real love," she sings at one point, tying reminiscence to the stuff dreams are made of.

At the same time, this song stays very much in the moment. "Is it dream or is it déjà vu," she and her backup singers ask over a slowed rhythm bed every bit as bouncy as what's come before. This song is a come-on. Blige uses her alto to growl over the qualities pulling her toward the man in the song, someone she may have just met out on the street but who evokes old memories.

A young Busta Rhymes (at this time known mainly as the scene-stealer on A Tribe Called Quest's "Scenario") introduces the next movement—the tale of a relationship that plays out over the bulk of the record, starting with a sexy cover of Chaka Kahn's "Sweet Thing."

That sexiness is one of the big differences in Blige's cover of the song and the original (cowritten by Khan and guitarist Tony Maiden). Though it's about forbidden love, Khan's record sounds like a sunny afternoon in the park; Blige's almost note-for-note re-creation conjures up a darkened bedroom. Some of that difference comes from subtle shifts in the arrangement—Khan's voice skips along with easygoing guitar and keys, while Blige's plays off hip hop percussion. But the heart of the difference is Blige's more guttural and urgent phrasing. Though from a neighborhood every bit as rough as Blige's, Khan did not grow up in the Pentecostal church as Blige did. Blige testifies, and she owns each word. You can listen to Khan's version and never quite catch she's afraid of going crazy; Blige turns the notion into a threat. Extending words into hollers and cries, she pushes her backup singers over the last minute of the song like her very soul's at stake.

Blige hangs onto that impulse for the jazziest track on this record, "Love No Limit." Improvising on the deepest colors in her alto, Blige sounds like the girl who caught people's attention singing Anita Baker. Still, where Baker's alto sax of a voice soothes first and foremost, Blige uses her distinct strengths and focuses on the struggle. Blige's song is a pledge of commitment—"Freely, completely, everything you want I'll be." It's a richly contradictory article of faith—absolute devotion to someone else as a form of freedom—and she wrestles to maintain that stance from beginning to end. Near the end, when she seems to grow tired singing her "loving you, babe" mantra, she goes into her more extreme vamps, her voice soaring high in a prayer for strength.

"I Don't Want to Do Anything," her duet with Jodeci's K-Ci Hailey (on a cut written and produced by the quartet's DeVante

Swing) provides the album's honeymoon moment. K-Ci's big gospel vibrato provides a perfect springboard for Blige's exuberant attack—a vocal that starts off sounding like she plans to tell the guy off and winds up exultant over the reciprocal commitment to the "Love No Limit" Part Two concept of the song.

It seems the lovemaking can last forever on "Slow Down." In the context of this album, this song forecasts the persona we will soon come to expect from Mary J. Blige. She's asserting her needs at the height of the album's most rhapsodic arc, and what she needs most is patience and attention.

Because both hip hop and soul anchor themselves in reality, it shouldn't be surprising that the album's relationship arc ends there. "My Love" kicks in with a strolling bass and high-stepping snare, the singer lamenting a love turned sour but also taking some measure of pride in how hard it's going to be for that ex to get along without her. This blues-based independence already suggests Blige won't settle for being another producer's protégée or a pop star also-ran.

The last blend of hip hop and soul here, "Changes I've Been Going Through," clearly comes from a woman who has only begun to mine the complexity of her character and her talent. She begins mourning a relationship that's "all gone." She rationalizes why this may be a good thing, but finds herself bargaining with her lost love before the end of the first verse. She then expresses anger over his inability to reciprocate her love. Against stuttering hip hop beats and some meandering piano and spiraling key figures, she denies the end and pleads for another chance. Four of the stages of grief may be whirlpooling into the abyss here, but this remarkably subtle and gorgeous vocal sounds like a woman who sees beyond her years.

That's before her sexy response to Grand Puba's closing pickup lines during "What's the 411?" This is the one straight rap cut on the record, and Puba spends his time on a classic brag—promoting himself as equal parts tough and lovable. Blige may not be much of a rapper, but she sells her rhymes by letting her personality shine through in the phrasing. She uses this opportunity to reiterate the key themes here—she needs her boundless love reciprocated, and if he's serious enough to walk it like he talks it, "I might just give you a call." By the time she's singing the cut's outro, "You're very special," she seems to be singing to herself, no longer concerned with Puba. The love letter is redirected to her audience. A growing number made it clear they were ready to answer her commitment with all the devotion she could want.

# 6

# Changes I've Been Going Through

Within a month of the debut's July 1992 release, Peter Watrous's "The Pop Life" column in the *New York Times* gave Mary J. Blige the title that would haunt her and goad her throughout her career. Watrous interviewed Andre Harrell, who said, "She sang for me in my office [and] I thought that she could become the queen of hip hop soul, which is exactly what she is becoming,"

In the same article, Blige explained, "I've been singing in church, around the house and in school. . . . I sang in the choir in my church in Yonkers, I sang lead and I could never figure out why the members wanted me to sing lead, but I did it." Soon after, she told *Variety*'s Denise McIver, "I still listen to old gospel more than anything. I was actually going to do a gospel song for this album, but we ran out of time." In a November *USA Today* interview with James T. Jones IV, she cited the recently deceased James Cleveland and the sometimes-crossover hitmaker Tramaine Hawkins as specific influences.

Watrous wrote, "There are thousands of churchgoing virtuoso singers, but they don't have Ms. Blige's sense of style or attitude. She's an around-the-way girl, a hip hop culturalist, and it shows in her demeanor."

Blige seemed to verify this, continuing, "There's nothing wrong with being hard-core. I grew up in a neighborhood where that's all there was. If people are looking for long dresses and high-heel shoes, they'd better look somewhere else."

This early candor suggested that Blige already knew her first job was to represent her people, those who hadn't been evident in TV or even heard on hit radio, at least since the soul era of her childhood. It also showed what culture shock she was about to face. Her album went straight to number one on the *Billboard* hip hop/R&B chart and number six on the Top Two Hundred. *USA Today*'s James T. Jones opened his feature, "Mary J. Blige, the queen of hip-hop soul, is the first to break into the male-dominated world of new jack swing. Her street-hip persona and deft combination of R&B vocals and hip-hop beats have put her in the ranks of Bobby Brown, Keith Sweat, Al B. Sure! and Jodeci. . . . Right now, she's reigning over them all." Quoted in that same profile, leading rap magazine the *Source*'s Chris Wilder stated, "She is Aretha to the rap generation."

In March 1993, she won the *Soul Train* best new artist award, but she also began to experience backlash to the hype. A *London Evening Standard* gossip column sneered, "Mary J. Blige, soul sensation of the States, is in competition for pop ego of the moment. According to our chums in the USA, Ms. Blige is causing all sorts of trouble with her suspect temperament." The *New York Times*'s Jon Pareles wrote, "Her voice is impressive, but her style doesn't qualify her to be, as she proclaimed, 'the queen of hip hop.'"

Then, in June, she received negative reviews for her first appearance at London's Hammersmith Apollo. She took the stage late, performed three songs, disappeared for fifteen minutes, and returned without explanation. She found herself booed upon returning to stage. The *Guardian*'s Caroline Sullivan ended her review with that moment: "Offering no explanation, she asked, 'Are you still with Mary J. Blige?' At that stage, frankly, no." London's *Times* ran the headline, "Mary, Mary Far Too Contrary," stating, "It is far too early in the game for this slight figure in the baseball jacket to be taking the sort of liberties with her audience that would make even the oldest hand blush." That event would haunt her next tour as well, when the same paper would refer to her London debut as a "fiasco."

Blige's brand-new relationship with worldwide media attention confronted her with situations she hadn't been prepared to face. She would soon be called out every time she was late to an interview and declared difficult when she reacted negatively to an interviewer's questions. She admitted later that she saw everyone as out to get her, and, to some extent, they probably were. It became evident that, while the press liked to celebrate a new soul singer for her "around-the-way girl" qualities, it didn't really know how to, or want to know how to, talk to someone from the hood.

Blige responded to all of the drama by reaffirming her roots. When she made that London trip, her record on the charts was "Love No Limit." The following fall, she released "You Don't Have to Worry," a one-off for the *Who's the Man?* soundtrack and a sizeable hit on the R&B charts and in the U.K. The video for this streamlined piece of funk—voice over staggering beats and little more than a trace of keys—shows Blige looking more hood than ever. She's dancing on a car surrounded by a block party or she's dancing on a stoop, alternately wearing various oversized (as in men's) jackets, jerseys, bandannas, baseball caps, and shades. She's singing a defiant promise. "You don't have to worry, I won't waste your time." She'd bring out one more single in the spring and the album to prove herself the following fall.

# 7

# Hip Hop a Go-Go

What Blige and Combs did with that first album had a big impact on a young producer from Washington, DC, Chucky Thompson. *What's the 411?* came out just when Thompson was beginning to understand the connections between DC's unique go-go movement and its national sister movement, hip hop. Blige's album convinced Thompson he had something to contribute to music outside of DC. In a 2013 interview with the author, Thompson talked about his growing appreciation of the connections between the cultures. "They used to have block parties with go-go, the same thing that happened in New York with deejays. The same stories I heard about New York matched up with what happened in DC. The thing is you're in the street, so if you're in the street, you're ready for anything to happen. You have to be good, or else.

"And *What's the 411?* hit me. I had a cassette copy I carried everywhere. Even though it was her record, it felt like my calling."

To Thompson's ears, Blige's record responded to what he had been doing for a while. "One keyboard that could do everything was an Ensoniq EPS, and I took that keyboard and just learned how to produce, but I was incorporating music that I was playing along with learning hip hop. At the time I heard the *What's the 411?*

album, it was almost like a stamp to say, 'Yeah, you're right on top, you're right there where music is right now, where music's going.'"

The fact that the call of Blige's record spoke so powerfully to an artist living in DC is significant because, in some ways, DC was (and is) one of the most "outside" urban areas in America. With a majority black population hidden behind a facade of neo-classic architecture and monuments to dead white men, it's easy to see why, in our interview, Thompson referred to it as "the most northern of southern cities." Like most DC youth in 1992, Thompson loved hip hop, but "Chocolate City," as locals had long called it, had its own musical genre, in many ways every bit as youthful and vital. Go-go developed out of funk about the same time as hip hop, both as a party-based reaction to the increased homogeneity of late-seventies mainstream R&B (a.k.a. disco).

Thompson explained,

> Go-go bands have a history of playing other peoples' songs. It started out as a Top Forty situation, so it became the deejay versus the band. When the deejay came with the cross fader, he could keep more people on the dance floor. [The Godfather of Go-Go] Chuck Brown's idea was, let me put a percussion break in between the songs, and that way I could keep people on the dance floor longer. Have a call and response—are you tired yet, you ready to go. That's how go-go evolved. But then the beats and the sounds and the percussion took on a whole new life.

In their 2009 book, *The Beat! Go-Go Music from Washington DC*, Kip Lornell and Charles C. Stephenson quoted Chuck Brown further explaining how he built new rhythmic possibilities out of pop record ideas: "At that time, all the disco beats was like 120 beats per minute . . . so we said 'We're going to chop that in half, 60 bpm, and slow that beat down and syncopate that beat so people can understand what's going on there.'" Having a background playing Latin music, Brown added horns, a variety of extra percussion instruments, including congas, and gave the music a beat-based groove with a difference. Brown's breakthrough single, 1978's "Bustin' Loose," sounded a little like some meeting ground between Earth, Wind & Fire, the Gap Band, and James Brown (though it has a long, fluid conga break unlike any of them). In other words, it connected several traditions in a unique way—not incidentally, a mix steeped in the sort of grittiness that set Blige apart.

---

Thompson's professional connection with Combs and Blige resulted from his decision to step outside of DC—"to the next town over"—and work with musicians in Baltimore. "It was a whole new world from DC, and I met a deejay from Brooklyn." The deejay introduced him to one of Sean Combs's new producers, Ward Corbett. "He let Puffy hear some of my tracks, and Puffy said, 'Yo, I want a meeting with him, and let's sit down and figure something out.'" Thompson went to New York to meet Combs. On that trip he also met Christopher Wallace, the rapper known as, alternately, "Biggie Smalls," "Big," and "the Notorious B.I.G." Thompson became excited about working with him as well. "Puffy had just been fired from Uptown, and he'd started Bad Boy. He tried to take Mary and Jodeci, but that wasn't working out. [Combs had a special arrangement with Uptown to produce Blige's *My Life*.] I had a choice between signing with Puff and Hiriam Hicks. Hicks could promise me TLC, but Puffy could get me TLC, Mary, and Biggie."

From the moment Thompson drove up to meet with Combs about Blige's record, it took on a life of its own, starting with Combs hearing the rough cut of the *My Life* music, a vamp on Roy Ayers's 1976 title track, "Everybody Loves the Sunshine."

When I got there, I was loading up stuff to see what it sounded like on his system, and he ran in and said, "Yo, make me a copy of that. I'm going to play this for Mary tonight." And Mary said, "I was just thinking about that [Ayers] record." All three of us at the same time, that song kind of emerged . . . before I even got there. I was just thinking, you let me trick it out and mess with it on a level that I don't think anybody would think about at all. It's definitely a Roy Ayers record, but it's also the way that I played certain things in there, where my mind was at.

Thompson explained further,

When I was building *My Life*, I was messing around with different timings. I programmed that song on the Akai MPC3000 [a classic hip hop sequencer/sampler], so it has different swings, and different things happen with those swings; so I swung it in a way where it fit where I was coming from and give it the feel that happens here. That's why it has a hop to it. I knew Mary was dope enough to catch that hop.

I was actually mimicking a [go-go] group from DC, Rare Essence. Those were my muses. I used to go see them faithfully, starting in the early eighties. They had the best musicians I'd ever seen in the world as far as the funk is concerned and as far as the sexiness of urban music. I was imitating Rare Essence and imitating Roy Ayers. At that time, I'm just getting into the game, you know. I'm very much a fan of Puffy's career, and him being so young and where he was. I was a superfan of Mary's. I wanted to throw a few things in there to see if they would become fans of mine.

The trio grew close, and even closer as Blige became good friends with Thompson's girlfriend. As they got to know each other, they uncovered more connections. "Mary's one of those people who knows every record that comes on quiet storm [radio]," Thompson explained, adding, "and I know them all too."

Thompson emphasized that in contrast to most of their peers, he and Blige also shared an appreciation of less New York–centric hip hop. "There's one particular moment that I remember sitting with her. We were at her house, and Bone Thugs-n-Harmony came on, 'Thuggish Ruggish Bone' [the crew's first single, which came out just months before *My Life*]. That girl, Shatasha, that part at the end, we used to always laugh at that part." The video is rural-industrial, and Shatasha's naming of the crew members and declaration that "Cleveland's definitely in the house" can certainly be understood as country humor, nowheresville humor. "Cool things like that helped me have a better connection to her. Most people from New York, they're into New York. There's no outside life after New York. Puff was straight New York; his vision and vibe came from Harlem, New York, but he had people like me, Biggie, and Mary who lived outside of that and helped stretch the vision a bit."

This artistic bonding sealed the deal on *My Life* when financial conflicts began to get in the way of the project. "Because of the success of the *411* album, they came back to the table with some outlandish numbers for the second album. Mary talked to Puff and said, 'Well, look, would you and Chucky like to do the rest of my album,' cause we were already making things happen."

Thompson had a vision of what Blige was capable of doing, and he wanted to help shift the media's perception of her.

> I just felt that she was getting the brunt of a lot of bad publicity, and I know that at that time of her life, she was from the hood, and a lot of us from the hood, we just don't take to that craziness. Also, it's easy to get caught up in that lifestyle. Beyond all of the negative press, a lot had to do with the way Puff saw her and envisioned her as a female guy, a little more urban than most R&B—she embodied that urban lifestyle. She caught a lot of backlash for that.
>
> But I saw the soul music, the talent, and I said, you know what, there's more to this story than people give her credit for. I didn't want to talk about it. I wanted to show her that I knew she was beyond what people were thinking that she was. That was the connection between the two of us.

Like others who worked with Blige, Thompson recalled how hard she'd work in the studio to get down exactly what she knew a record deserved. "On 'I Never Wanna Live without You,' she got real emotional when we were making that record. I could hear her crying in the booth, but she wouldn't stop. Even though she was going through what she was going through, she was still professional, she was still an artist. She just pushed through. There was a lot of stuff that we had to go back and do other takes, that she wanted to re-sing. It was mostly her saying 'keep that' and 'let's take it back' to get that vibe she captured on that record."

Though Thompson downplayed his role, he had something to do with every aspect of *My Life*'s production, starting with playing every instrument on fourteen of the seventeen cuts and contributing some instrumentation to all of them.

Herb Middleton had a couple of songs on there, where I came in and just added some seasoning to what he had. I also worked with Nashiem Myrick doing looping and all that. Puffy had most of the pressure to deliver this album, and he knew where he wanted to go, but I would be on the side just coming up with stuff. The more I would hang with her, the more I would get to know who she was, the more I would see her talent, the more I'd go, "You know what, let's see if she would like this." That mentality of jacking records [i.e., sampling] was still there, except that I played instruments, so I could jack a record and give it a whole new life. We were still in the culture of what was happening, but I wanted to bend it a little bit. Make it a little bit more personal, you know.

If one thing sets *My Life* apart from *What's the 411?*, it is indeed how personal the record feels. To this day, it is not just the favorite record of most Mary J. Blige fans, but it is the one they call theirs. Of course Blige herself, as a singer and now also as a writer, was at the heart of that intimacy, but central to this defining platform for her voice is the art of collaboration. Unfortunately, the individualistic image of stardom, along with enormous changes in technology, has too often obscured the collaborative side of pop music over the past two decades.

In his 2013 book, *Mo' Meta Blues*, the Roots drummer Questlove writes, "The day that Mary J. Blige's 'My Life' came out in

1994, we all just sat in the van scratching our heads. We had never heard anyone sing over samples before, and here she was, with Roy Ayers's 'Everybody Loves the Sunshine' under her, making up a new vocal, new lyrics. We were so caught between rejecting it as untenable and accepting it as the vanguard."

Though that reaction no doubt represents a common response to Blige's defining moment (and some of its importance), it misreads what Blige and Combs actually achieved on that record. And it completely overlooks the role of Chucky Thompson, soon to be dubbed "the classic" producer for a number of different artists, beginning with Usher and the Notorious B.I.G. and including many key women—Faith Evans, Mýa, and Mariah Carey as well as New Orleans artists Juvenile and Ledisi. As for Blige, in the coming years, she continued to bring Thompson in for key cuts, with or without Combs.

# 8

# My Life

Between the time Mary J. Blige released her first album and her second in November 1994, the pop charts changed. R&B now dominated hit radio, and women dominated R&B. Blige played a distinctly important role in this insurgency of women's voices, placing six singles on the crossover charts as the most gospel, most street-savvy of her contemporaries. For the first time since *Billboard* began compiling annual charts, half of 1994's Top Twenty singles featured women artists, six of those artists black. A quarter of the year's Top One Hundred singles came from black women artists. By comparison, at the height of the 1960s "Girl Group Era," that number never topped 15 percent.

Blige occupied a unique position in the group of acts that included both veterans and newcomers, a new set of girl groups and seasoned R&B divas. TLC defined the nineties hip hop/R&B girl group while, for a long moment in '93 and '94, SWV stormed the top of the charts with silk spun lighter than air. Janet Jackson, Mariah Carey, Toni Braxton, CeCe Peniston, Zhané, and Crystal Waters all presented themselves as uptown sophisticates. A slew of first-name-only newcomers, Brandy (Norwood, age fourteen), Monica (Arnold, fourteen), and Aaliyah (Haughton, fifteen), were precocious as hell but still novelties thanks to their youth (however, before long, all three would begin to work territories dovetailing different aspects of Blige's world).

This emergence of black women's voices took place during a time of great change in popular music. Radio formats shook from the impact of a new generation of country singers dubbed Young Country as well as the seizure of hard rock formats by a vanguard of post-punk rockers from Seattle sporting larger-than-life production values formerly associated with heavy metal, earning a new label, grunge. These two new forces, as well as perhaps a perennial industry fear that pop radio was getting too black, kickstarted a trend toward more narrowly focused radio markets.

In the midst of all this turmoil, Mary J. Blige's *My Life* established several things at once. First, it featured Blige's writing credit on fourteen of the seventeen cuts, establishing control by the artist over both her message and her revenue. Second, it merged the hip hop grounding of *What's the 411?* with the musical ambition of soul's great concept albums, particularly those Marvin Gaye classics, 1971's *What's Going On* (arriving the year of Blige's birth) and 1973's *Let's Get It On*. This connection between Blige and one of the great auteurs of soul music made a claim for her cultural significance, furthered by her commercial success. The album itself stayed number one on the hip hop/R&B chart for two straight months. *My Life* is the record that truly earns the queen her title.

---

As with the first record, *My Life* opens with a phone call from Combs, but this time, Blige answers quickly. When he asks her if she's ready, she sounds confident, self-assured. Cinematic strings drape the return of a champion.

And this champion's grown up in more ways than one. While *What's the 411?* courted the listeners with romance before launching into its sexier material, "Mary Jane (All Night Long)" starts things off in the throes of passion. A strong bass pushes forward against strings sexy enough for "Let's Get It On." "Let's make love like we first met," a sultry Blige proposes, working in the themes of the previous record—remembrance and commitment. Blige laughs and skats and sounds for all the world like she's matured ten years in two.

On the verses of "You Bring Me Joy," the pulsing funk carried by both the bass and Blige's voice call to mind Prince's club hit "Gett Off" from three years before. Blige sings alongside a chorus of women, adding a tribal feel to the pulse. Horns chime as it builds. The end effect might be that of a seventies disco phenomenon if there wasn't a certain menacing unpredictability to the playing and singing. The ecstasy promised in the opener has become overwhelming.

"Marvin Interlude" makes it clear those earlier strings were no accident—with Blige's layered, wordless vocals overtly tipping the hat to the master of the soul concept album. The groove of "I'm the Only Woman" delivers Blige's familiar theme of commitment as a meditation. She's the one who's made this mistake. And her vocals yearn to untangle a complex web hung with triangle, wah-wah pedal, and strings. She insists her lover not let her go, but pounding piano and pulsing percussion offer only bravado against uncertainty.

That meditation sets up the album's title track, something qualitatively new from Blige. Blige's first overt "message song," "My Life" works like a sort of sermon in reverse. Bassist/coproducer Chucky Thompson has replaced Ayers's three-chord upward progression of bass and keys on "Everybody Loves the Sunshine" with a bass-dominant step up, back and partway forward again. Ayers's transcendent meditation, even rooted as it is in pain, has hit rockier ground here.

After declaring her authority—"If you looked in my life and see what I seen"—Blige spends two verses asking her listeners to learn from her, to be honest and speak their minds, to be patient and persevere. She offers belief in God as part of a series of options (belief in her story, belief in each other, belief in one's self), whatever it takes, to gain the time, clarity, and patience to accomplish one's goals. It's a restrained record, Blige's vamping kept to a minimum, her final words of encouragement designed to soothe. This is a record about keeping a useful focus.

The next two cuts, produced by Herb Middleton, offer the album's most ethereal, quiet storm moments. Both secular devotionals, "You Gotta Believe" features Blige promising (especially forcefully after an interjection by on-again, off-again real-life boyfriend K-Ci) that faith in her love will be rewarded, while "I Never Wanna Live without You" finds Blige's own pledge of dedication fading into the backing vocals provided by Faith Evans. Interesting that producer Chucky Thompson particularly remembered her struggle to record this one because what she was after was a tough trick, a kind of noble loss (heightened by the fact that Blige has admitted she felt threatened by Combs's increasing focus on Evans).

The album's climactic performance, "I'm Goin' Down," threatens to plunge her into the darkest places she's gone yet. As Rose Royce singer Gwen Dickey did on the Norman Whitfield–penned 1977 original, Blige caresses each word of the lonesome quiet moments, just her voice against searching high notes on guitar and two keyboard notes beating like a slow-moving clock. Then, she drives the music hard when horns, strings, and rhythm guitar punch the chorus home. The big difference in the two records is subtle, but profound. While Dickey sounds agonized and sad, even weeping in the record's final third, Blige sounds like she gains strength from the pain. In the process, Blige makes Rose Royce sound as present tense as any of the many James Brown "Funky Drummer" samples on any given rap record. In her loneliness, she may be losing her mind, but she's also finding herself through the process of singing about it.

The following "My Life Interlude" reminds us of the overarching soul suite taking shape on this record, and she comes back fighting in yet another love song, not unlike the ones that preceded "I'm Goin' Down." But this one, "Be with You," is musically harder hitting—with both jazz and funk elements, slamming drums, and those gangsta keys made popular by Dre and Snoop Dogg ringing in some late night/early morning vigil. The infectious groove of

"Mary's Joint" carries the fight forward, backing vocals asking, "Why can't we work it out, oh baby, can't we try," while the singer builds her case despite a series of promises broken.

By the next song, "Don't Go," he's out the door, Blige conjuring and pleading for it not to be true over snippets of harp, disembodied voices, and harpsichord-like keys. A conjuring is beginning to take shape that breaks forth in a mystical reverie with "I Love You." Voices swirl around Blige's vocals, which themselves begin to take on the form of an incantation, repeating "I love you" over mysterious horns and high-pitched electronic tones. From the beginning, *My Life* has echoed Marvin Gaye's form-defying, album-length meditations on sensuality and spirituality; at this point, it becomes an extension of Gaye's work, from a woman's point of view.

The last-ditch appeal of "No One Else" uses hip hop samples, scratches, and blasts of sound over a slightly menacing rhythm bed to reach a funky groove reminiscent of another great soul mystic, Stevie Wonder.

The album closer (and the album's first single), "Be Happy," couldn't be a more complete homage to the album artistry of Marvin Gaye. It starts with ocean sounds and seagulls before flute and strings begin a cinematic build. A popping bass groove propels the song forward, wind and rain and ocean swirling in the keys and strings that surround it. Blige begins asking how she can love, "When I don't love myself enough to know when it's time to go." After a tug-of-war of emotions (she still takes moments to tell the man off and remind him what he's missing), Blige wills herself to move on with her life. As on many a Gaye record that followed *What's Going On*, Blige's lead vocals sing with and against her own whirling backing vocals. This song, ultimately about her search for self-love, answers "Real Love." The optimistic bounce of her first big single is gone, but it has been replaced by a tougher, yet equally irresistible groove and a more focused idea of just what that love may be.

# 9

# Natural Woman

With *My Life*, Mary J. Blige became a more substantial artist, a young woman with a distinctive style who could shape the world around her. You can see it and hear it and feel it in her video for the lead single "Be Happy." In the videos on her first release, Uptown seemed to struggle with ideas about how she should be presented. In "You Remind Me" and "Real Love," she alternates between dressed-up sexiness and tomboy sports gear. For "Reminisce" and "Love No Limit," she sticks with high-end sophistication.

It didn't take Uptown long to figure out Blige's own style was a synthesis of these tendencies. That's when Andre Harrell dubbed her "ghetto fabulous." The "Be Happy" video uses the style to make a statement. Opening shots focus on a sparkling vintage condenser microphone, with high-contrast glimpses of Blige rocking to the beat. While singing, she's only seen in fragments, but everything about her is radiant. She's classic; she fits that mic. When the camera pulls back, it's a kind of reveal, though her eyes are still obscured by sunglasses.

She's wearing a metallic puffy jacket, large hoop earrings, and any number of shiny rings on her fingers. The image alternates with her in a black leather jacket and cabby hat. She's down to earth, and she's bigger than life—ready for the street, block party, limo, and stage. While she's singing, her voice soaring, her expression edges toward a smile. In the shades-off shots of her sitting and thinking, she seems far less certain, wishing and hoping . . . perhaps for the listener to answer her call, perhaps for the music to carry her away.

Tapping into the current of African American culture that resists binary thinking, "Be Happy's" image of "ghetto fabulous" replaces the either/or with the both/and. All of the videos for the *My Life* album benefit from this coherent sense of Blige's aesthetic, her fashion sense a near-perfect complement for her musical sensibility, her rootedness key to her flight.

Since some of the early press on Blige emphasized her lack of professionalism, the push with *My Life* promotion was to show Blige ready for the world. No doubt following a training model set down by Motown, Harrell sent Blige to an artist development company, Double XXposure, for a twenty-four-week course in etiquette (a class she later admitted she left after seventeen weeks). In her March 1995 interview with *Essence*'s Deborah Gregory, she was already talking about "her 'unprofessional' era," when she used to show up late and snap at reporters, and this theme that all of that was behind her dominated press from this period (with the occasional slip, such as her August snap at *Ebony*'s Touré, answering one of his questions with, "What do you think?," then calling him "stupid" and ending the interview).

One substantial difference in the interviews this time around was that she was clearly more comfortable talking about herself. She explained her prior irritability, in part, as a symptom of the helplessness she often felt in the hands of others, including her record company. She told Gregory, "You have to pay back every dime that your record company invested in you before you see a penny. As hard as I worked, I wasn't making any money sometimes. And I wasn't happy about that at all."

She admits that she got tired of the same kinds of questions in the past, particularly those about her boyfriend, K-Ci. In October 1995, she told *Ebony*'s Muriel L. Whetstone, "I don't really like to be asked who I'm sleeping with." She then added, "If you were in my shoes, would you want someone to ask you a bunch of personal stuff about you and your man?"

In that same interview, she was also quick to correct assumptions about her music and redefine it as she saw fit: "*My Life* is not an autobiography. It's just music. Every single day is what my album is about. Every time you walk out of your house, that's what my album is about." She told Whetstone that writing the record was important therapy for her. It's an important distinction because *My Life* is very short on narrative and long on meditation, the actual tale of Blige's life more implicit than explicit, as are the connections with fans abstract rather than concrete.

Blige was emerging as something much more than Combs's protégée. In her interviews, she emphasized her writing on *My Life*. Those songwriting credits (where artists tend to make the most money from their material) meant Blige was taking more control of her career. Though she didn't yet have production credits, Blige's role shaping the sound had also become evident. In December, writing for the *Baltimore Sun*, J. D. Considine stated, "Unlike a lot of singers her age, Blige refuses to let her producer do most of the work. . . . Good as the grooves are, it's her vocal work that ultimately drives these songs."

Her next single, released on a soundtrack EP for the Fox TV show *New York Undercover* (a show coproduced by Andre Harrell and King of the Cop Show Dick Wolf), upped the ante on that vocal work. She covered a record many would rather have left alone, Aretha Franklin's 1967 single, "Natural Woman." Jerry Wexler's production of Franklin's version of that Goffin and King song is a thing of unearthly beauty, a cathedral of space that can only be made intimate by Franklin's warmth. Blige's version is a reverent tribute, only slightly modified by Blige's tendency to work the beats a little harder. The most positive addition to the original may be a playfulness to Blige's version, particularly in her call and response with the backing vocalists. This notion is amplified by the song's video, which features the band dressed as a wedding party, the lead vocalist playing the bride, and backup singers decorating the notes with Supremes-like arm choreography. But what matters most in terms of Blige's career is simply that this version is passable, a meaningful accomplishment honoring the greatest voice of the soul era. (In 2003, at BET's Ninth Annual Walk of Fame Tribute to Aretha Franklin, Blige would do even better—singing directly to Franklin, and comfortable enough with her own gifts to give the song some Pentecostal push at the close.)

But it was "I'll Be There for You/You're All I Need to Get By," the duet Blige released with Method Man in late spring of 1995, that fixed her role in hip hop history. It's almost surprising today to see this record as the springboard for a Stephen Talty article in the *New York Times* defining "The No. 1 Summer Song of Love," especially since *Slate*'s Chris Molanphy, nineteen years later, would claim Talty's article "cemented" the link "between summer and hip hop jams." When we think of hip hop summer singles, we typically think of sunny songs—DJ Jazzy Jeff & the Fresh Prince's "Summertime," Tupac's "California Love," or Daft Punk's "Get Lucky" (even the year of the Method Man/Mary J. Blige single, the more obvious choice is Shaggy's "In the Summertime"). "I'll Be There for You/You're All I Need to Get By" is anything but sunny.

Sure, it begins with that shiny Ashford & Simpson melody, made famous by the most radiant duet pairing imaginable, Marvin Gaye and Tammi Terrell, and that's what Blige sings, Tammi Terrell's part, throughout. But Blige is moaning over her own vocal, and she's singing the Motown lyrics slowed down, wistful, plaintive. The keys are eerie, the beats insistent, and the bass menacing. In the video for the single, the tone is desperate; the couple huddles on a roof, jonesing for some kind of fix to the situation, hanging onto each other in the meantime. But the strongest emotion evident in both song and video is that the couple have a bone-deep appreciation for one another, are equals in their triumphs and their troubles. When Method Man says, "You my nigga," he's saying he couldn't better appreciate the woman there by his side, huddling against the darkness.

It's this groundedness, this blues sensibility and working-class consciousness, that seems consistently to carry Blige through her darkest periods. The summer of 1995 was one of those. Faith Evans's upcoming August release featured *My Life*'s production team of Combs and Thompson, all under the umbrella of Combs's Bad Boy Records. And, though Combs had just told Scott Poulson-Bryant, "The stuff I've created with [Blige] is the best of my whole life," Blige knew she was losing her standing with him.

Even as "I'll Be There for You/You're All I Need to Get By" sat in the *Billboard* Top Ten, Blige took a hard hit from an unflattering profile by Veronica Webb in a July 1995 *Interview*. The story portrayed her as an enabled drunk, and Blige, who thought she'd had some understanding with Webb, felt betrayed. Still, Blige would later characterize this moment as a personal bottom in terms of her drug use.

Shortly before, on June 30, one of Blige's great inspirations, R&B singer Phyllis Hyman, died of an overdose in her New York City apartment. Hyman had worked some of the same musical territory Blige worked—from early seventies soul (when she started) to her last crossover hit, the new jack "Don't Wanna Change the World." In 2000, Blige told *Ebony*'s Kevin Chappell, "[The day Phyllis Hyman died] I said, 'I'm not doing this anymore.' [Hyman] was so beautiful. That was the day when I said 'no more. No more. I can't do this anymore.'"

Though it was two years before Blige released another record, she kept her nose to the grindstone, working on herself and her music. At the beginning of 1996, her single for the Babyface-produced *Waiting to Exhale* soundtrack, "Not Gon' Cry," soared to the top of the R&B charts, eventually hitting number two on the *Billboard* Hot One Hundred. A year after that, she performed the nominated song at the Thirty-Ninth Grammy Awards celebration, in a medley alongside Whitney Houston, CeCe Winans, and Brandy. Amongst these three princesses, Blige again defined the ghetto fabulous, with her long, silver coat, matching silver pants, dark shades, and bright, large rings on her fingers. And the urgency of her vocal truly set her apart. She pulled enthusiastic applause from the crowd, exclaiming each word, "I should have left your ass a long time ago!" When she returned to the stage at the end of the medley, joined by all of the other stars from the project, including Aretha Franklin and Chaka Khan, she looked shy, but she also looked formidable—Method Man's tough-guy equal and a natural woman all the same.

# 10

# Share My World

Reflecting the deepened maturity of "Not Gon' Cry" as well as the optimism of her March 1997 single, "Love Is All We Need," Blige's third studio album featured a set of arresting portraits by a young photographer named Kevin Westenberg. The cover art for April 1997's *Share My World* showed a singer not only more sophisticated and uptown than ever, but also warmer and more inviting. Even hiding behind Fendi shades, Blige seemed down-to-earth, and her clothes looked soft; there was room next to her in the backseat of that car on the back cover.

Having broken with Sean Combs, Blige risked becoming less accessible. In interviews, she had often said Combs was the one who knew how to give her audience the musical hooks they wanted and needed. To the extent that is true, *Share My World* is all the more remarkable because it is filled with hooks that sound unaffected and purposeful. Blige makes full use of the opportunity to turn loose from some of the barriers of a tough-girl pose and reaches for a wider spectrum of sound, including more tender shades of emotion. Key to this working, Blige's gospel impulse, rooted in secular concerns, was now beginning to bloom.

And the timing was right for Blige's broadened reach. For the first time, Blige wasn't going up against her girl group competitors TLC (themselves dealing with management problems capped by bankruptcy), and she took center stage in terms of the crossover potential for the intersection of hip hop and R&B. She made the most of it, taking on the finest producers in her field: the team behind Janet Jackson, Jimmy Jam and Terry Lewis; the man behind everyone from Pebbles to Toni Braxton and the force behind the *Exhale* soundtrack, Babyface; Aaliyah's R. Kelly; as well as artists she knew well, like Poke and Tone of the Trackmasters, who produced both "Be Happy" and the Method Man duet; and some important newcomers, Rodney "Darkchild" Jerkins (who had worked with Vanessa Williams before and would wind up by Blige's side through the rest of this story) and an up-and-coming rapper named Jay-Z. Blige rekindles a Stylistics hook and covers Natalie Cole, calling to mind virtually every era of soul—more like a sunny Stevie Wonder record than the relatively dense Marvin Gaye thickets typical of *My Life*.

Ironically, or even more likely by design, Blige's breeziest, most pop outing to date came during a very dark period for rap music. The hype around the media-embellished "feud" between East Coast and West Coast rappers had reached two tragic endings. Tupac Shakur blamed Combs for five bullets he took leaving a recording studio in 1994. Rumors then flew that Combs believed Shakur had an affair with Christopher Wallace's (a.k.a. Biggie Smalls) girlfriend Faith Evans, and the press circulated rumors implicating Combs's Bad Boy Records in Shakur's murder in Las Vegas in September of 1996. Smalls was shot to death in a Los Angeles club parking lot in March of 1997.

Blige had been friends with Smalls (who got a second stage name, the Notorious B.I.G., from his role on a remix of Blige's "Real Love"), and Combs's focus on Evans is one reason Blige gave for striking out on her own. Perhaps because of so many close connections, Blige hasn't ever talked much about the events surrounding this supposed East Coast–West Coast feud. Many fans doubted this war of words was actually what caused the rappers' deaths, and with the gritty realism of both rappers' art and Shakur's revolutionary politics—only a few years after the Los Angeles riots—people whispered about possible FBI involvement behind the troubles. Someday, Blige may offer her point of view on all of this, but it's safe to say her personal accounts of her drug use and relationship problems during the era suggest she was now mainly trying to gain control of a crazily spinning life. *Share My World* revisited Blige's consistent themes of commitment and redemption with a greater vision—one of new multicolored vistas and something like newfound peace.

Though this was her first number one album on the pop charts, the album was less successful with critics. Some saw the use of multiple producers as a loss of artistic focus, Blige's voice all but buried in the production. This response may have had more to do with an antipop bias among music writers than it had to do with the quality of her work. Some fans of her first two albums wanted Mary J. Blige to remain a harder alternative to more confectionary sounds like those associated with TLC, Janet Jackson, and Mariah Carey.

But all these years later, *Share My World* holds up well, with some of Blige's finest vocals to date. Her second Babyface collaboration, "Missing You," makes a "Not Gon' Cry"–sized leap in maturity and impact—her aching voice sailing above a gospel chorus woven out of multiple tracks by both Blige and Shanice Wilson.

What most matters about *Share My World* is the way Blige's voice serves each song and the way each song serves the whole. After some dramatic proclamations about Blige by Rich Nice— "the most innovative female singer of our decade"—that seemed to drive critics crazy (most of whom, it must be considered, could not hear those claims as the audience heard them, in a nineties climate where fame tended to run its course much faster than the five years Blige had been on the charts), Blige opens sounding both older and sexier than ever before. With the line, "I can love you better than she can," Blige recalls the promise she's made since her first album, singing over sister LaTonya's backing vocals and Lil' Kim doing what she does best—rapping tough and taking control, in this case, alongside a provocative bass figure.

With huge bass and drum flourishes that pan back and forth

in the mix at the end of each refrain, Jimmy Jam and Terry Lewis almost overwhelm Blige's more girlish-sounding vocal on "Love Is All We Need," but her struggle to stay afloat in rough waters makes the song all the more compelling. Love may be all we need, but that doesn't make things easier. Perhaps because Blige is trading in one production team for new partners, community is a key theme on this album (as it should be for a Queen of Hip Hop Soul), and it's telling that Blige sounds most cool and confident after rapper Nas, who pretty much defined "street cred" at the time, jumps in with a responding call to "stay strong."

Though "Round and Round" features the new Trackmasters production team, and it's built around an early DJ Premier and Shawn Carter (Jay-Z) sample, the song's an album highlight because of Blige's voice. Singing with her own backing vocals, she drags out the title phrase as if she's spinning on a Tilt-O-Whirl, trying to figure out a relationship that's turned bad on her, not asking to be let off so much as cautioning—"Where I stop, you will never know." With George Pearson's keys lighting the carnival, it's both hypnotic and emboldening.

As it should be, the title track is warm and generous—sharing, bigger than life. Guitarist Michael Jordan plays rising arpeggios that punctuate each refrain like gravity-defying drops of dew. Bells ring in the mix. Bright organ pulses for a moment and vanishes. All the while, Blige sings both backing and lead vocals. She pleads with the listener to stay in her world, promising "a brighter day." That balance of desperation and vision gives the song its tension.

Blige's performance of "Seven Days" earned New Jersey songwriter and producer Malik Pendleton an American Society of Composers, Authors, and Publishers (ASCAP) award. Built around the days of the week, the song turns another Tilt-O-Whirl relationship into an infectious sing-along. Quietly simmering production gives Blige room to work her lower register and deliver emotional depth to the simplicity. The last of the album's five singles, this is the most explicit in its ambiguity.

Blige's following duet with R. Kelly, "It's On," is the polar opposite, a decision to jump feet first. Blige's sandpaper vocals scuff

Kelly's silk, speaking of pain and more than a little fear even as she tries to believe. Perhaps that fear explains why she stops and says a prayer of thanks before moving forward.

Banged piano chords announce the next song, simultaneous with the opening line, "I'm not in love." Thus begins what may be the album's finest new track. Babyface-penned "Missing You" is a gospel-style build featuring layered vocals by Shanice Wilson, who plays a one-woman choir. Ascending bass and wah-wah guitar punctuate a slow march toward clarity. "Missing You" is secular gospel at its finest, the individual coming to grips with the truth that it's okay, moreover it's good and necessary, to reach for love. Individual strength and love for another do not have to be at odds.

"Everything" shows just how far Blige can reach. Built around the Stylistics track "You Are Everything," this is a sunny track, swirls of sitar and bell held together by bass. Though both sentiments and production threaten to spin cotton candy here, Blige improvises frantically, sweating and shouting to keep her feet on the ground. The results are both physically intense and epic in sweep.

The magnitude of everything demands Blige's call to "Keep Your Head," as she sings in the following song, cowritten with sister LaTonya. Blige called this her favorite song on the album, and it's telling. On a record full of spectacular mixes, this is built around a spare hip hop pulse with a motivational refrain and vamp on top. It's all about being grounded while standing tall. Sisters together call for listeners—and presumably each other—to keep their heads high, repeating, "I don't need to tell you why." Though the message can and should be tied to both civil rights and feminism, it is also very personal for these sisters and their audience, a durable rudder for rough waters.

The next two songs keep to this sleek, funky vein. The singer's dreamy, relaxed vocals over the tinkling piano and washing harp in Rodney Jerkins's spiraling groove of "Can't Get You Off My Mind" suggests she may just be ready to give in. On the Wonder-ish "Get to Know You Better" (produced by Bryce Wilson of Groove Theory), Blige displays the confidence of a woman who feels she has a few things figured out. Though she sounds cautious, when she begins to sing the "la la" refrain of Wonder's "My Cherie Amour," she leaves little doubt that she's moving forward, whatever the dangers may be.

The jazzy "Searching" (Blige scats here before it's all over), built over Roy Ayers's vibes from the song of the same name, links the singer's personal problems to a larger world where people hurt each other because they can't connect. Pulling lyrics from the Christmas carol "Do You Hear What I Hear?" and the spiritual "Mary, Don't You Weep," she finds the problem of love tied up with a lack of unity. By singing "I'm not trying to preach to you/I'm still searching too," Blige appeals to listeners to help her find the answers.

What follows is indeed unifying. Blige plays it straight with a modest update (by producer James Mtume) of Natalie Cole's terrific 1978 pop single, "Our Love." As with her previous covers, what Blige lacks in terms of the technical graces of the original singers, she compensates for with the grit and integrity that makes her distinct. And there's a certain democracy that comes with that too. Blige sounds like a sister, down to earth and walking right beside you. Even before the exultant build at the end, it's hard to find anything in Blige's canon that testifies more emphatically to the glory of love's promise. And it's "our love" that's being celebrated here, taking each listener firmly into its embrace and urging her (or him) to sing along.

"Not Gon' Cry" closes the album and opens the way for Blige to play a mature woman. It's a classic Babyface anthem, with the title as a compulsively singable refrain. As Babyface did with Karyn White in 1988, he elicits a performance that seems beyond the singer's years. In this case, the at most twenty-five-year-old singer cries out about this relationship she's put up with for "eleven years," and we don't question the numbers: we feel our hearts break, and we cheer her on. This is Blige's first Sunday morning confrontation song, and she not only sells the emotions in the song—the self-righteous anger that will allow her to make this break—but she seems to take on weight with the song, each line having a density and a center of gravity that soon became core to the story.

# 11

# On the Road with MJB

## ALYSON WILLIAMS

On the cover of her 1989 debut, *Raw*, Alyson Williams's golden eyes drew the majority of the camera's focus, while she stood tall, (at least) as regal as Queen Latifah, wearing a leopard-skin pillbox hat, matching gloves, and a black cape over a black suit. That cover still announces hip hop and soul, and no single figure worked that territory so definitively as Williams in the three years before Blige's debut. There were, however, crucial differences between Williams and Blige. The daughter of big band leader Bobby Booker, Williams had been exposed to a wide range of talent and techniques unavailable to a young Blige, without the rootedness in the Pentecostal church. All of that perhaps guaranteed that although Williams served as a vanguard for territory she calls "hip hop R&B," Williams moved on to other forms of jazz and R&B, while Blige was built to develop a blend of hip hop, gospel, and soul that would help redefine the meaning of "popular music."

When I talked with Williams in 2013, those eyes still shined with all of the fire captured in that album shot. Standing as tall as Blige, she was just as regal as ever. She was also remarkably warm, fortunately open and candid about the hip hop soul she helped create. Having worked as a vocal contractor for Blige, she had vivid memories of the inside at a time when the young Blige was struggling to find a way to live in the realities of newfound stardom.

Williams remembered the first time she worked with Blige.

Mary was about to go out on the Budweiser Superfest with Bone Thugs-n-Harmony, Ginuwine, Dru Hill, and Aaliyah, and I had gotten word that they were auditioning background singers. They had auditioned all the Lisa Fischers and the Cindy Mizelles [these first two made famous in the 2013 film *20 Feet from Stardom*] and the Audrey Wheelers [famous for working with everyone from Madonna to Melba Moore]. . . . They didn't want to pay any money, but they wanted that caliber. Kern Brantley was the musical director, and they were rehearsing the band—they were great. Mary was in Europe. She'd be back on Monday, but they still didn't have any singers, and this was Wednesday or Tuesday. So I called the manager and said, "This is Alyson Williams, and I understand you're still looking for background singers. You're not going to pay for Lisa and Audrey and them, so what are you going to do?"

He hems and haws and puts me on pause. And I said, "This is what I propose. I can get you some background singers, and I'm sure you'll be able to get them at the rate you're trying to pay. I will come in as the vocal directress and pull the girls together, and I'll tour with you, and you know, you work it out with me 'cause I'm basically saving your ass."

So he put me back on hold.

And he comes back on, "So when can I see 'em?"

I went and swept up my two girls. They were working at the Motown Café, when that was still around off Fifty-Seventh Street. Mitch Matlock and Inga. And I stuck them in the back of my hooptie with a tape recorder and got them learning songs. And we went to the audition and pulled it off.

Williams remembered being frustrated by the way Blige was being produced.

What surprised me was that, with all of this production they were putting behind Mary, I thought that when I saw her she would have come out of that little shell where she was. They had dancers, four or five female dancers and five male dancers, and I kept trying to interject things that I knew about the stage.

The choreography was in place. But Mary still wasn't comfortable in her skin. This was 1997, *Share My World*. They had dancers and things, and they had people to lift her, and all you could see in her face is "please don't drop me" instead of living in a lift. [Williams raises her arms in the gesture of the dance.] You know what I'm saying. You have to live in that. It's not by accident that Beyoncé can be put in a harness and be swiveled down from the ceiling. They've been training that darling to be swiveled down from the ceiling. And she's ready for it now that she's had the opportunity to do it. I would be ready for it because I've looked forward to flying across the stage like Barbra Streisand in *Funny Girl*. That's what I watched growing up, and that's what I wanted to do.

As Williams touched her breast, reflecting on this dream, it was apparent that she would do that job brilliantly. It was also apparent that Williams had different ways of hooking an audience, or a single listener in an interview, than a Mary J. Blige might have. Williams is self-aware in her embrace of theater. Blige's theater, in the main, started with church training, and movements away from a naturalistic sense of reality are greeted with suspicion. That's not to say Blige is less self-aware than Williams, so much as it is that Blige knows the unique demands of her appeal, caught up in a sense of her as an everyday woman. To some extent, Mary J. Blige could not be an everyday person without embracing the role of diva as it was handed to her, but she had to do it in a way that allowed her contradictions to stay in play.

To the extent that hip hop itself charted new territory, Blige had to tackle every challenge without clear road maps. Naturally, the ones that were handed to her did not grasp her dilemma nearly so well. Williams reflected on the difficulties the production style created for Blige.

> It was very difficult for Mary to have such a big production put around her when she didn't feel worthy or ready for it. It was very rough. She had her sister [LaTonya] out on the road with her. She had a few other people. I just thought the whole management team was a problem.
>
> She had her cousin with her, and he was a real strange little guy who had just served his bid, and he was angry with everybody, and I guess he was doing the best he could to protect his cousin, but he was just angry, you know, and just mean. You can't have mean people around you 'cause they will make you mean. Your people have to be a reflection of you and still get the job done and be a deterrent to hanger-ons or whatever the case may be. And I just got the feeling that . . .

Williams paused, thinking about how best to capture the whole of their relationship, including the problems she had trying to do her job as well as she knew she could.

> There must have been a little intimidation there. But it was never meant to be, because I was there to do a job. I was Alyson Williams, singing background for Mary, it was my job.
>
> They were glad I was there with her; she was glad I was there with her (she told me how she used to sing "Just Call My Name" into her hairbrush in the mirror), but I think some of them may have felt like I might overshadow her.
>
> But I know how to fall back. And I was trying to work with their vision and give the backup singers things to do, and they were shutting it down. And it disappointed me because I had already gone to see Luther Vandross and all these other people, and she might not have done things as elaborate as that, but your whole stage has to move and complement you. The band is going to do what they're doing, but you can't have three people

just [standing there]. . . . We're supposed to support you just like the dancers do. It doesn't have to be elaborate, but it has to be something.

Williams has a big sisterly quality, almost maternal. As she talked about the (slightly) younger singer, her eyes shined with warmth and compassion. She wanted it to be clear that she respected Blige then, and respected her even more two decades down the road.

In the latter eighties, whatever was going on between women and R&B and hip hop just became more defined. We all suffer the same thing . . . and we minimize ourselves and we are victims of things that leave us feeling that we are less than we are. So Mary took up the gauntlet of "I'm going to tell my story and let you see that I'm just like you. And that I've survived it." And, as she continued to grow, she came with the *No More Drama*, and she started to find herself, and she would put it on record.

But Blige still had a sharp uphill climb ahead in 1997. Williams said,

She was nowhere near the singer she is now, then. And even now, my critique for Mary, and I'm not hating or saying anything that I wouldn't say directly to her, there are still some areas where she can be a little flat and sharp at the same time, something I call "flarp." For the most part, she's found range, and she's found how to approach a note. She now knows how to sing. She just continues to learn how to sing well consistently. 'Cause there are a lot of people who can sing, but they don't know how to be consistent. They just open up their mouths and sound comes out. But when you know how to use your voice and use your breath, and enunciate and use your teeth, your tongue, and your lips and your vocal—it's all those things that make the sound and make it happen. She didn't know that. I know she had people with her who were supposed to be coaching and teaching her that.

And not unlike sentiments I heard from others, Williams expressed frustration that Blige had to learn so much the hard way.

They did *The Tonight Show*. The day of *The Tonight Show* became my actual last night of the tour. The day we were scheduled to be gone, that week, I was scheduled for a play. The play was rehearsing out of L.A., which is where the last dates were. At the end of the time, they got a date for her to do Jay Leno. But I said, "I have to go to rehearsals earlier that day, so I'll meet you at NBC Studios," or wherever it was, and they got all up in a bunch, but I was like, "I've got something else on my schedule. What's the worst that could happen? I know my notes, I'm the leader of the vocals. . . . You don't have to worry about me. Just trust that I'll be there when we're ready for taping."

That wasn't good enough for them. I don't know how they related it to Mary, but I'm sure it wasn't related the correct way. So when I got to NBC Studios, they were like, "No, we're not going to need you, blah blah blah blah blah." And of course I wanted the airtime, and I wanted the salary.

But everything wasn't for me. So I went on back to the hotel. And I waited until eleven o'clock. They took her out to buy something real nice to wear. She was wearing a nice Chanel pants suit; she looked impeccable. And this guy came in from New York who used to work with her, and they had him coaching.

So this is what happened. Mary came out and did her little scared performance, because she always looked scared back then. But she sang it down! And the band was great!

Now, you're standing on the dais with Jay Leno, and he will shake everybody's hand when he goes down. He said, "Don't forget to pick up *Share My World* from Mary J. Blige, we thank her," and all of a sudden her arms crossed, and she decided she was going to step off the stage and go straight towards the camera. . . . The way she'd been staged that was the only door she knew to come through.

And I was sad they didn't catch it. And I said, "Who is it who can go out and buy her a suit and fly somebody in to supposedly train her, but you can't tell her protocol and make her comfortable enough in her own skin?"

No doubt there's plenty of blame to spread around regarding the troubles Blige faced in the first decade of her career. There are also lots of reasons to cut some slack. After leaving Combs, Blige was charting unknown territory without the assurance of her surest navigator. The fact that she survived is remarkable. But she did so much more than merely survive, and her greatest achievements still lay ahead of her.

# 12

# The Tour

In 2006, Mary J. Blige told journalist Gavin Martin she'd like to destroy all existing copies of her 1998 album, *The Tour*. On the other hand, in his "Consumer Guide" column, veteran music journalist Robert Christgau called *The Tour* "where to begin" if one wants to appreciate Blige's music. Blige's concern about the set is with her voice, which had grown much stronger and more controlled by 2006. But as Christgau wrote, "If her raucous tone and sour pitch aren't deliberate, they aren't unwitting either—she believes, correctly, that her fans will relish them as tokens of honesty." He then added a line that sums up what Blige has absolutely come to stand for: "And to go out she covers Aretha's 'Day Dreaming,' which made clear long ago just how street soul sisters on both sides of the monitors really want to be."

Christgau's choice of "Day Dreaming" underscores one of the things that sets Blige apart from most other contemporary female singers. She's not afraid to express a desire for traditional notions of romance. That honesty is part of what keeps Blige in direct contact with her roots in the street. Most of her immediate precursors went out of their way to distance themselves from what could be interpreted as weakness.

Janet Jackson, Pebbles, and Jody Watley sang, respectively, about being in control, driving the Mercedes for the boy, and looking for a new love to replace this unsatisfactory one, but Blige can often be found begging to relinquish control. While her rivals TLC may not be too proud to ask for what they want sexually, this live set underscores Blige's desire for something potentially more revolutionary. As a girl who's grown up rough enough to know she has to take control both in and out of the bedroom, Blige daydreams of a world where she might just catch a break, in life and love.

The sequencing of this live set is all about the never-ending love song at the heart of Blige's career. She opens with a promise to spend the night searching for "Real Love," and then pursues that love through the sentimental connections in "You Remind Me," "Reminisce," and "Sweet Thing," which she follows with the conviction of "Mary Jane (All Night Long)" and "Love No Limit." On one level, the show is the call for unity articulated in "Searching"; in some ways it's the arc of a romance novel.

To move from a focus on *What's the 411?* material to *My Life* material, the band plays, the choir sings, and Blige vamps over a few bars of Kool & the Gang's "Summer Madness" before taking on the more complex reflections of "My Life" and the more urgent call for conviction in "You Gotta Believe." Interestingly, the *411* album's most overt call for control, "Slow Down," comes at this point in the set, followed by "Mary's Joint," which begins with that concession, "I know that you're just a man."

This is when the fight for romance goes gloves off. "Now ladies," Blige shouts, "tonight, if you all feel like you're the only woman out there that can't no other bitch fuck with you, let me hear you scream!" An ecstatic crowd roars back, and "I'm the Only Woman" reveals the anthem at the heart of each of Blige's pleas for love. Of course, it doesn't hurt that the backup singers, warning "Don't be a fool like your daddy," make it plain the groove guarantees women have the upper hand.

There's a version of the Mary J. Blige story that wants to reject *Share My World* as a failed step away from the hard street grooves her fans loved her for. That's the version that makes her seem to apologize for the record when she sings "MJB da MVP" almost a decade later, and that's a rap version of history that's not far removed from a punk or metal version of history—the harder the music the better, the more raw the more real. But that version is belied by the live crowd reaction to the opening salvo from the *Share My World* album, the sweetly phrased guitar intro to the title track. At the sound of those notes, the crowd screams louder, in more instantaneous unison, than at any point before.

And then they quiet down, because it's a quiet song, and you can easily imagine the female-dominated Universal Amphitheatre crowd rocking side to side. That same exuberant approval greets the refrains of "I'm Goin' Down," again exemplifying the strength in vulnerability uniting this crowd. In "I Can Love You," after Lil' Kim's rap, when announcer Benny Pough begins repeating, "Do the ladies run this motherfucker?" the answer is clear.

The point is made so completely, in fact, that male backing vocalist Dustin Adams takes the lead on "Keep Your Head," without changing the feel.

In the end, she makes sure this is a true post-Combs show, featuring seven songs from her breakaway album, dropping only one of the hits and adding both the title track and the great non-crossover single "Missing You." The final run-through of original material—"Everything," "Seven Days," "Not Gon' Cry," and "Missing You"—is a hook-laden sing-along, very feminine and all the more powerful for it.

Still, the songs are redefined. Blige turns "Everything" into a love song to the audience, thanking everyone from her individual fans to the radio stations that play her records. "Seven Days" becomes a street-smart explanation why this woman is so hesitant to let her friendship with this man go any further. "Not Gon' Cry" becomes a unifying anthem—"He wasn't worth it, was he, ladies? We're not gonna miss him . . . fuck 'em," she tells the crowd. But then the show closes with "Missing You," confessing and embracing the truth that what really binds us together is our pain. Blige begins stomping and shouting, "Do you miss Tupac tonight, y'all? Do you miss Biggie Smalls tonight, y'all, yeah? Do you miss Eazy-E, yeah, yeah, yeah?" And the crowd cries back, raw gospel call and response.

Which brings us back to "Day Dreaming," one of two covers that may or may not have been actual encores but work like them on record. "If my mother was out there, I'd dedicate this to her tonight," Blige says before singing Dorothy Moore's 1976 hit version of "Misty Blue." Blige gives the end a slow gospel build, improvising, thanking the audience again and telling them, "And if it was you, I'd be out there screaming and cheering for you."

# 13

# Sisters in the Studio

## CHANNETTE AND CHANNOAH HIGGENS

Across the continent from Blige, Channette and Channoah Higgens grew up in South Central Los Angeles. From their earliest memories, the twins wrote songs, rapped original rhymes, and impressed those around them with their harmonies. Their mother had been a songwriter, taping her song ideas and soliciting her daughters' support as background singers. After a while, she couldn't find the tape recorder because the girls kept taking it— they had so many ideas of their own.

Seeing Michael Jackson in *The Wiz*, they were fascinated with him and talked their mother into buying *Thriller* when it came out. As they grew older, they fell in love with New Edition, and they cite Babyface as another key influence. Buying his *Tender Lover* album and seeing that he wrote and produced all of his own material inspired the girls. Channette once told a group of firemen visiting her school, "I want to be the biggest entertainer, composer, producer, songwriter, singer, rapper, dancer in the world."

Starting with their families and their classmates, the girls performed for virtually everyone they met. By high school, they were being invited to work on classmates' musical projects. They also played area talent shows. At one such show, Motown music executive Cheryl Dickerson liked what she heard. Soon, they were playing with New Edition's Ricky Bell. However, New Edition had recently reunited, and it left the girls underused, forcing them to break with Bell, a move still painful for them. They began composing melodies and lyrical and vocal arrangements for other producers' rhythm tracks; writing for 702, Immature, Blaque, and Mýa; and creating a remix for Destiny's Child. They soon began working with Danish producers Soulshock and Karlin.

In our 2013 phone interview, their warmth and exuberance leapt the thousand miles between us, making me feel like a familiar and welcome friend. Though Channette seemed the more chatty of the two and Channoah the more reserved, when they got talking, they all but finished each other's sentences, their twin conversational style as engaging as the hooks and harmonies they brought to Blige's fourth studio album.

Channette Higgens started things off, recalling the day their work with Soulshock and Karlin led to working with Mary J. Blige. "Karlin would be on the keyboard and freestyling, they'd start singing, and he started playing the beginning of 'Memories,' and I started singing through that. Channoah suggested, 'Let's do this for Mary J. Blige,' and Karlin jumped at the idea."

This wasn't the first such suggestion.

We had probably, for a whole year, with other producers, been saying, "Can we do a song like Mary J. Blige?" So up to that point, we'd done about seven songs for her that she just never heard because these producers were not big enough or whatever, but we'd been writing lots and lots of songs in the Mary J. Blige vein, to get to her.

So I'm thinking, "She's never gonna hear this," and I don't know how we came up with the concept, it was about Valentine's Day. We never write about holidays, but it was just coming to us very easy. . . . We just put the vocals down, and we immediately switched to another song.

But then we come in one day, and they say, "Guess what? Mary J. Blige is doing the song!"

From the moment Blige said yes, the Higgenses found things moved differently than how they'd come to expect. "They said, 'We want you guys to come down to the studio,' and that was new because usually the artists did the songs when we weren't there. They said that she wanted to change some lyrics. Now, that didn't throw us, so we said, 'Okay.'" In fact, as they tell the story, it seems evident that this opportunity to meet a hero was more exciting than anything else.

But there was tension that came with the excitement. Channette recalled, "There were some people in the studio who scared us, saying 'Well, you know, be aware of Mary, she can sometimes be a diva, and she has an attitude.' We were like, 'Really?' And they were like, 'Yeah, just be careful.' So I remember thinking, 'Well, I'm from the hood, Mary J. Blige is from Yonkers, which is the hood. Mary J. Blige is us. We got it.' So we were like, 'Let's say a silent prayer that everything goes well.'"

Together, they seemed to remember every detail of the day they met Blige.

Now it's time for us to drive down to Westlake Studios, and we're very nervous because we understand that we are meeting a straight-up hip hop and R&B legend. We love Mary J. Blige. She is the representative of R&B and hip hop music married to beautiful melodies.

We were going, "Oh my gosh, we're driving down to the studio to meet Mary J. Blige? And she's going to do our song?" Again, it was one of those surreal moments. We had many of those in the industry.

Our manager was already at the studio, so we meet him, and he says, "Yeah, she's in there. So get on in there, guys, she wants to talk to you girls to change some lyrics."

So here we go, we're walking in. And I see her, and she's sitting with another lady next to her, who I thought, rightly, was her sister LaTonya, and we go, "Hi, nice to meet you, my name is Channette."

"And I'm Channoah," her sister chimed in. Channette continued,

Then she goes, "Oh my gosh, oh my gosh, you guys are twins!"

And I'm looking at her because she's dressed so stylish. She has black leather pants on with this white top, and this black-and-white leopard print cowgirl hat, and she's just sitting and styling with this big hat on.

And we had black leather on too.

She said, "I love the fact that you guys are sisters and working in the industry. This is my sister," and she introduced us to her.

Now, we are the type of young ladies that, if we admire someone, we are going to tell them that we admire them. So we kind of give a big speech to them. "We just want to tell you that it's an honor for you to do our song."

And she said, "Well, it's an honor to meet you because I loved your demo. I'm doing this because of your demo. I was listening to it on the plane, and I love you guys's voice."

We said, "Thank you."

But Blige wanted to make some changes, and she took time to talk them through with the young women. Channette recalled the subtle nature of these changes.

She said, "I love the part 'We're all alone on Valentine's Day,'" and I think the lyrics were, "I really want to call my girls, but they're probably gone anyway." She wanted to change that to "I really want to call him up, but my pride is all in the way."

I can't remember what our lyrics were to these other sections, but she wanted to change the line "Vision's getting clearer, I see what's been going on for years," and she wanted to change [it] to that line at the end, "The ones you say are far really are so near."

Channoah stepped in,

She was so cool and so down to earth, I was comfortable enough to say, "I don't understand that lyric. I don't get it. What do you mean by that?"

And she said, "I mean, you know, he's not here, but he's in my heart." And we said, "Oh, okay. That's cool."

What shocked me was that here was this legend, and she was so humble that she was worried that she was changing our lyric. We told her, "Now this is your song too, so we want you to be comfortable."

That's when she told us that she already had another song on the album about holidays, and she wanted to change the lyrics to emphasize the differences.

Channette continued,

I remember asking her, "Do you want to go over the song?" And I remember thinking in my head, "What if she says, 'No, I got this.'" But she was like, "Okay!" And we came in and played the song, and we went over the change of lyrics, and we're all singing together and hearing this legendary voice, and I'm thinking, "Am I in this life?"

She was completely willing for us to vocal produce her in those moments. And she took direction. She had no ego. All this warning of "Be careful because she can have attitude," and she was nothing but the sweetest, coolest, down-to-earth, almost like a little lamb because she was just like a kid, you know, "Show me how to do it." It was just like, "Show me how to do this, ladies."

It was a day of unexpected turns.

I remember Soulshock and Karlin coming in the studio at this point, and they're meeting her, and she's meeting them, giving them a hug and everything. And we give them a hug. And we were telling them we were going over the song, and she said at this point, "When I get in there, into that booth, I'm going to really kill the bridge." And we said, "Yeah, yeah, girl, you're gonna kill that bridge." I guess she's talking about how it changes over to drum and bass, and she's like, "I love that!" And she claps her hands and says, "Okay, I'm ready to go in," and she goes into the booth.

This was our cue to leave. We thought we were not going to be allowed to stay in the session, and Mary yet surprises us again and says, "I want the girls to stay. Can you guys stay?"

We say, "Yeah, we can stay!"

She said, "You guys wrote it, you guys are singing it, show me how to do this." Not to disrespect Soulshock and Karlin, who did the beat, but she was saying whoever did the vocals and sound like that, I want you to stay. She then made the reference that she wanted to keep us on the background. She was like, "I want you to keep the girls. I'll do a couple of their main notes, to blend in with them, but keep them on."

Channoah felt like they needed to share that moment with the woman who got them started.

I got sort of overwhelmed because we were with Mary J. Blige in the studio, and we were close with our mom, so I stepped out of the studio to call my mom. Just to say, "Mom, she's doing it, and she sounds great!"

And she's recording the whole song down, no stopping, even if she messes up, even if she forgets a lyric, they're just recording her all the way down, and she's doing it really good, and I'm just amazed that she's giving us this much props. After about two hours of her being in there doing it over and over again, we get a call for another session and we end up leaving. She's still in there with Soulshock and Karlin, going over it again.

But the story wasn't over. The time the women had spent in the studio before Soulshock and Karlin came in had set up yet another chapter. Channette said,

I remember asking, "So are you almost done with the album?"

She makes a face and goes, "Mmm . . . pretty much. They want me to do this other song, but I'm not feeling the demo."

We said, "Oh really?"

She said, "Yeah, they want me to do it, but I don't know if I want to do the song."

I remember telling her, "If you don't feel it, don't do it, you know?"

She says, "I know, I know."

That was in the middle of the session. About five days later, we got a call from Randy Jackson, the vice president of MCA Records [the well-known judge from *American Idol* who has had a successful thirty-year career as a session musician and producer], and he says, "I need you guys to do me a favor."

We said, "What?"

He said, "Diane Warren [who has written hits for everyone from Celine Dion to Aerosmith] wrote this amazing song for Mary J. Blige. It's called 'Give Me You.' I think she just does not want to do it because of how the demo singer is singing it. If I could shoot this tape over to you, and you guys could listen to it, change whatever melody, change whatever, just make it Mary J. Blige."

We said, "Okay, give us the tape."

We put it in, and I'm floored because the demo is like, you picture a young white girl in a choir, and I know Mary J. Blige is not going to sing that, you know? And at the beginning . . . "I don't know too many things" [singing high, stiff, and enunciated], and Mary J. Blige wouldn't sing it that way. Mary would go [dropping her voice and giving it a swing], "And that is you, baby, next to me, but I'm satisfied." This young girl singing it, I can understand why Mary thinks, "I'm not going to do it." So we go in the studio a few days later with Diane Warren and Randy Jackson, and we do things the way Mary would do them. We did melodies and kind of changed things. We did the whole song, "Give Me You," not knowing it was going to be a single. It was a trip to hear later on. Mary heard it after we did it and said, "Okay, I'll do the song."

So we didn't get any credit on that, but the album comes out, and Randy Jackson calls and says, "Guess what, I'm going to make your song the next single!"

We said, "What!" And we were all happy and jumping up and down.

And he said, "No, 'Give Me You.'"

And we said, "That isn't our song."

But the Higgenses didn't focus on the downside of things for long. The whole experience was a fond memory.

We were so proud when it came out. It was so crazy to look on the credits. And I remember hearing that Mary called her management, and she said, "How do you spell their names again?" She wanted to make sure she gave us special thanks.

Never, ever listen to rumors, because here she was humble, willing to take direction from us, asking for our permission to change the lyrics, wanting us to stay in there to give it direction, giving us props, calling back to make sure our name was correct, telling her entourage about us, I mean a lot of positive things that she did that we will never forget.

# 14

# Mary, the Album

One way Mary J. Blige signals that she is indeed an artist who thinks in terms of albums (someone who crafts a collection of songs to be heard together) is through her album art. *Mary*—all stark black and white, featuring the title in cursive font and Blige's left profile—makes a bold visual statement. Before this moment, the public Blige wore hats and sunglasses, with her hair combed down to obscure the scar under her left eye. That scar is featured prominently as a piece of this portrait of the artist, her hair and necklace just barely in frame. She looks more mature than before— regal in her simplicity, calm and soulful. On the back cover, her long locks and charm-laden necklace give her a sophisticated, bohemian look.

And that new look is telling because, between Blige's third and fourth studio records, a friend from South Orange, New Jersey, all but stole her title. Lauryn Hill of the Fugees had worked on a remix of "I Love You" from *My Life*, and, building on the reputation she had earned covering Roberta Flack's "Killing Me Softly," Hill launched a solo career firmly rooted in the early seventies soul sounds that informed Blige's music.

There were, however, significant differences in the two artists. Compared to Blige's tough upbringing, Hill came from a middle-class family, her mother a teacher and her father a computing systems consultant, and Hill began singing and acting on stage at a young age. In high school, she formed a hip hop group with a Haitian American friend, Pras Michel. Eventually, with another friend, Haiti-born Wyclef Jean, they formed the Fugees, an act that featured a hip hop mix of Caribbean rhythms and soulful singing and managed to sell over six million records by the time Blige released her third album.

When Hill released her solo debut in 1998, she was accomplished at both rapping and singing. *The Miseducation of Lauryn Hill* was an astonishingly ambitious and tasteful synthesis of thirty years of soul, her biggest hit, "Doo Wop (That Thing)," deliberately nodding to the early-sixties doo-wop revival. Hill sold eight million copies. Of the R&B divas in the hip hop era, only Whitney Houston, Mariah Carey, and the girl group TLC sold more records, but they were all seen as pop artists first and foremost. TLC's strength and limitation (as with Aaliyah and the up-and-coming girl group Destiny's Child) was that they were always perceived as girls. Blige and Hill were the women of this musical moment, along with a handful of others who were not quite as popular—Erykah Badu, even more bohemian than Hill, and Faith Evans, who was essentially Combs's replacement for Blige.

Now, Mary J. Blige would not be the artist she is if she gave undue credence to such concern over her place in the field of show-biz divas, but she also wouldn't be the artist she is if she ignored it. She grew up singing call and response in the church (as well as hearing it everywhere around her in pop music). She responds to Lauryn Hill's call with, yes, a more bohemian image but, more importantly, an album that aims for an audience her own age—not Lauryn Hill's twenty-three but her own twenty-eight, an age not so much for experimentation as for making tough choices about the direction of one's life. The result is her first studio album to not reach triple platinum or have a single Top Forty hit. At the same time, it's the first album to be an across-the-board critical favorite. Both responses make sense—the album makes profound breaks with the past, all admirable if not necessarily friendly to Blige's fan base.

---

Perhaps more savvy than modest, one of the most interesting moves Blige made was to break her pattern and open the album with a song she didn't write. Lauryn Hill wrote "All That I Can Say" and provided the backing vocals. In that way, Blige embraced the musical moment and allowed the rest of the album to define her voice in contrast to Hill.

That said, "All That I Can Say" is a somewhat strange choice for opener. It's a mid-tempo, Stevie Wonder–like reverie with all of the mystical abstraction of a song like "As," which Blige had just covered with George Michael on his greatest hits collection. Unlike "As," which is frenetic and mind-bending, the Hill song is dreamy and contented with its ability to luxuriate in the idea of love. As with the first half dozen cuts here, "All That I Can Say" concerns itself more with grooves than hooks and takes shape in a way that defies expectations.

A series of cameos weave through this record, but aside from climactic appearances by Aretha Franklin and K-Ci Hailey, they don't call much attention to themselves. Yes, Elton John's piano groove from "Bennie and the Jets" is all but distractingly present on "Deep Inside," but he doesn't change it up. He pretty much samples himself, and the effect is Blige contemplating the troubles of success over a keyboard riff that screams "rock stardom." On the Diane Warren–penned "Give Me You," listeners notice Paulette McWilliams's airy backing vocals and Manuel Seal's warm organ long before they begin to suspect Eric Clapton is stoking some of the coals.

In June 2000, Blige told *Ebony*, "The Aretha Franklins and the Elton Johns. They didn't have to do it. It surprised me. It shocked me that Aretha would want to be on my project because I'm just a little girl compared to the time she's had in the music business. It made me really happy. I was like 'gosh!' I must be really reflecting something positive from the inner for those people to want to be on my album."

Of course, what Franklin heard in Blige had been there from the beginning—most prominently on the soul-searching of the first album's "Changes I've Been Going Through" and then, more explicitly, on the cover of Franklin's "Natural Woman," released on some versions of *My Life*. Blige was the young pop artist closest to navigating the territory Franklin knew all too well, between the demands of the mainstream and the raw truths of gospel, particularly using that forum to express the truth of a black woman's experience. No one else had done it better, and at this point, Blige was the same age Franklin had been when she recorded "Day Dreaming." It's hard to imagine two more sympathetic artists, even if we didn't know what we do about their turbulent relationships—Franklin's with her first husband, Ted White, and Blige's with K-Ci Hailey.

On *Mary*, Blige weaves a tapestry out of the connections between Franklin's emergence and her own era. "Beautiful Ones" samples Dionne Warwick's 1969 "April Fools," this Chucky Thompson production paying tribute to those great Burt Bacharach/Hal David records all but forgotten in popular culture. It's a delicate arrangement—all halting guitar arpeggios, swirls of harp, and winsome choral flourishes—working like bas-relief to emphasize the varied textures of Blige's alto. That same late-sixties pop feel characterizes "I'm in Love," with Thompson again providing key elements—percolating horns, sweeping strings, sophisticated backing vocals, and urban sax. Taken together, these two songs could be called pastiche if Blige's raw edge didn't make them sound so new. Blige is listed as sole producer on "I'm in Love," and an argument could be made that she's threading the needle here—one-upping Hill's synthesis of thirty years of black pop with songs like "Doo Wop (That Thing)."

Another Stevie Wonder cut, "Pastime Paradise," plays a prominent role in "Time," also coproduced with Chucky Thompson. Built around the rhythmic pulse and the melodic core of the original, the connections are made explicit in the final verse when Blige sings her lyrics over the easily recognizable bridge. At this point, Blige's call to end the dog-eat-dog gains urgency and depth coupled with Wonder's appeal to living in the present and facing a long litany of challenges in front of us. The politics of Blige's music continue to step forward—from the defiance in "Keep Your Head" to the call for unity in "Searching" to, now, a warning that "time is not on our side."

That statement made, Blige's collaboration with the Higgens sisters, "Memories," arrives as the album's first traditional pop song, in that it's straightforward and catchy. Though it's the most techno cut on the record, its bright, bold melody is almost as irresistible as the silky backing vocals. There's nothing thematically new here—it's a brokenhearted love song with a call to "move on," but the feel of the song is fresh—not wallowing so much as luxuriating in the details that still cause pain.

If *Mary* the movie were made, the following scene would show big sister Aretha knocking all such mementos out of little sister Mary's hands. "Don't waste your time!" Franklin declares, naming the track. "Stop making truth out of his lies," she wails, and it doesn't take long before Blige moves from questioning the advice to singing the refrain arm in arm with the undisputed Queen of Soul. That collaboration bolsters Blige for the confrontation with K-Ci Hailey up next on "Not Lookin.'"

Defending himself, Hailey's gravelly vocal opens "Not Lookin.'" Blige is not having it, and over seething, minimalist production, her voice grows stronger the harder she shuts him down. She's "sick and tired" of dealing with his lack of respect and calls, "All my ladies, stand up and clap if you feel me." When she closes, telling her real-life on-again, off-again boyfriend, "I know you're sorry," the effect is devastating, as in triumphant.

What follows is an unforgettable four-song sequence dedicated to women's independence and unity, starting with "Your Child," a highlight of every tour to come. The arrangement for this Gerald Isaac–penned song is minimal, placing emphasis on the power of the vocals. The refrains demand a sing-along as this woman conveys her respect for the woman who gave birth to her man's baby. "Gotta face reality," she sings, taking firm control of a heartbreaking situation. Most remarkable is her emphasis on sisterhood between presumed enemies. It can't be a coincidence that the most singable line is "Girlfriend, she wasn't disrespectful."

To underscore that empathy, she plays the "other woman" on the next song, "No Happy Holidays." Though produced by relative newcomer Kiyamma Griffin, this seductive jam could be a Babyface standard or one of those great records Jam and Lewis produced for Cherrelle. Though it's sexy, it's ultimately a lonesome meditation on a dead end—"Your family has never met me, and you've never met mine."

Jam and Lewis themselves return for "The Love I Never Had," a showstopper that anticipates the great success this collaboration would have two years later with "No More Drama." "The Love I Never Had" is "gotta face reality" unpacked. Blige starts off speaking over organ, and her moaned vocalizing contemplates the task ahead. The song is all contrasts—dreamy R&B verses followed by explosive gospel refrains. She stays present throughout all of that whiplash, gospel growling and even scatting to find her way through. After shouting, "I gotta wake up," you believe her when she cries it's "as painful as it seems." The now familiar Mary J. Blige laugh, from the gut but a little self-conscious, closes the track—saying "Ain't it true, and ain't it ridiculous too?"

Past the turmoil, Diane Warren's "Give Me You" starts with Disney-esque, morning-after strings, a french horn, and a harp. Of course, as syrupy as this song's dream of love may be, Blige's vocal sells it. She sings low and close to the heat coming off producer Manuel Seal's organ, offering every bit of the warmth she desires. Again, the call for romantic commitment feels less idealistic (or old-fashioned) than determined and even visionary.

A bid for commitment and community closes the album, another cover version sending listeners back to the tradition that gave birth to Blige's music. Great session singers Audrey Wheeler, Sharon Bryant, Cindy Mizelle, and Paulette McWilliams join forces with Blige to pay tribute to Philadelphia trio First Choice's 1977 oft-sampled dance hit, "Let No Man Put Asunder." The first three minutes re-create the original, but at the point when that

Salsoul track shifted into overdrive, all of the singers in the group goofing with each other and celebrating the moment, Blige seems to wind up alone. "C'mon, y'all, help me out," she almost whispers. Getting buried in the mix, she growls, and her energy fades, and all that talk of independence threatens to come to a sad end. Then she grabs the mic close and promises, in a voice as tough as any rapper, "It's not over."

# 15

# No More Drama

Though *Mary* was a critical favorite, it was the first of Blige's studio albums not to go triple platinum, and it was the first without a Top Forty single. And that's not too surprising when *Mary* is played against the body of material she'd previously released. *Mary's* maturity comes at the expense of youthful exuberance, and the hip hop influences are all but absent. Meanwhile, over on the pop charts, women singing hip hop–laced R&B were seizing the day.

Seven years her junior but an influential peer of Blige's since her debut in 1994, Detroit singer Aaliyah had two huge crossover hits at the end of the decade, "Are You That Somebody" and "Try Again." Her sinewy vocals played over Virginia Beach producer Timbaland's innovative rhythms, and her upcoming self-titled album promised to start the new millennium with Aaliyah a key player in the synthesis of hip hop and R&B. At the same time, the even younger trio Destiny's Child [featuring the ferocious lead vocalist Beyoncé Knowles] clearly held the pop music throne with six Top Ten singles between 1998 and 2000, four of those spending at least a week at number one. On the pop charts, only former Mickey Mouse club stars Christina Aguilera and Britney Spears had similar success.

Ironically, the pop success of hip hop/R&B hybrids did not necessarily bode well for black music labels. When I talked to Jeff Redd, he recalled, "A lot of these labels were getting rid of black music. I was at MCA for six years from 1996 until they closed that door in 2003, and the last two or three years before they closed, they were talking about, 'R&B is dead! Hip hop and R&B is dead!' And they had some of their biggest records around that time, like 50 Cent's 'In da Club.'"

All of these forces could have put Blige's career in a tenuous position in 2001, but the cross section of artists involved and the artistic integrity of *Mary* helped Blige work a number of different fronts at once. She seemed to be everywhere as the century turned. In 1999 alone, she played the Grammys, the Rock and Roll Hall of Fame, the MTV Video Music Awards, and the Essence Awards, and Whitney Houston brought her out to duet on Aretha Franklin's "Ain't No Way" for *VH1 Divas Live 2*. In October, she was featured alongside Bob Dylan and Sheryl Crow (among others) in Eric Clapton's fund-raiser for his Crossroads Centre drug and alcohol rehabilitation residential facility. In March of 2000, Houston presented Blige with the Soul Train Sammy Davis Jr. Award for Entertainer of the Year.

In the summer of 2000, Blige received a formidable list of favorable reviews for her sold-out concert tour, *The Mary Show*, which featured a projected superhero cartoon of Blige created by Stan Lee. In August, she told *Jet* she was donating proceeds from the tour to the 100 Black Men of America mentoring program for young men and women and to AIDS outreach in the black community. She was also involved in the Redeem the Dream civil rights march of that year and Rock the Vote. She even made her first movie, *Prison Song*. With the press, she was talking about sobriety and a more settled future, and she was thinking big about the possibilities of stardom.

In January of 2001, Blige took time out from working on her new album to perform "Walk This Way" at the Super Bowl with Nelly, 'N Sync, Britney Spears, and Aerosmith. Blige's fifth studio album promised to be her biggest record yet. But from the moment it arrived that August, *No More Drama* made it clear Blige intended something more. It marked the moment when an artist began to find a way forward past all of the career paths taken before her. The many ways the album spoke back to the musical moment—both in Blige's career and in the musical form she forged—suggested a great deal of close listening to others, including her fans.

*Mary* had been such a sobering record, with a distinctly troubled ending, that Blige told Australian journalist Kathy McCabe (in an October 2001 interview) fans had been asking, "Is Mary okay?" She meant for *No More Drama* to be a strong positive answer, and from its opening trumpet salvos and staggered wall of percussion (something like Death or God knocking at the door), the answer rang clear.

That first cut, "Love," heralds "the loving of a lifetime," and it comes in each verse's face-off with a former lover and choruses of determined self-talk. It's a noteworthy track in part because it features Blige collaborating with her brother, Bruce Miller (today a hip hop singer-songwriter/producer called CoraSon the Great, a nod to their mother built into that name). With her older sister LaTonya coproducing, her brother at her side, and K-Ci Hailey behind her, Blige sounds stronger than ever. As the backing vocals shout out the letters in the title, the inescapable image is Blige shadowboxing as she takes the stage.

Notably, this is all prelude to "Family Affair," Blige's first number one pop hit, and her first song seemingly made for the club. When you consider Blige's relationship with her audience during this period, it's worth noting that the *Mary* material's most significant play had come in the form of dance club remixes. (This new success in the club also affected the revision of this album five months in—a dance remix of "No More Drama" was added and the cover switched from a ghetto chic portrait of Blige with gold hair in a gold fur jacket to a new picture of her in red leather and red shades, looking for all the world like a dance club diva.) An insistent beat by West Coast producer Dr. Dre and another cowrite with Miller, Blige's New York brother, further underscore Blige's call to stop the hating and begin trying to love one another. When she shouts, "It don't matter if you're white or black, let's get crunk 'cause Mary's back," the word "crunk" even serves as a shout-out to the most vital and influential hip hop scene at the turn of the decade, southern rap. Even if "Family Affair" has personal meaning because brother and sister are working together on several of the key tracks on this album, the song is a clear call to a larger musical community.

And the song's so damn catchy in part because it's relentlessly playful. Blige makes up words anyone winds up singing along with by the second refrain—"Don't need no hateration, holleratin' in this dancerie!" By the third verse, Blige's vocals even begin rapid-fire slithers and slides that sound like rapped scatting. Nothing since the first album's "Real Love" had sounded so effervescent.

The 2002 revamp discards a couple of cuts about celebrity drama in favor of a song about community—"Rainy Dayz," Blige's hit duet with Ja Rule. As with Method Man before him (and as with 50 Cent later), Ja Rule's raw vocals strike a warming fire next to Blige's, which sound sprightly by contrast. Extending the psychological liberation of "No More Drama" into a more general call, the duet itself serves that end, as do the repeated calls to "smile for me." Even more, Blige highlights community by lyrically checking TLC's "Waterfalls" (no doubt due to the Irv Gotti track originally being destined for the trio) and Marvin Gaye's "What's Going On" as the guideposts we should recognize.

Blige hits southern blacktop when she joins hands with Virginia Beach's Neptunes (featuring an up-and-coming Pharrell Williams) for "Steal Away." This slinky fantasy about ghetto escape starts with Williams's quirky falsetto, which Blige echoes in that rough-edged way she has, bringing the rubber to the road. Marshane Smith's climactic rap, along with Williams's quiet assurance that "Mary got the gangsta lean," makes it clear that, though Blige may be done with, as she put it in "Not Lookin'," game-playing, "egomaniac, egotistical, chest sticking out, think your God's gift to me" thugs, she hasn't turned her back on her ghetto roots . . . or the corollary, the never-ending struggle to overcome the ghetto's limits.

The reworked 2002 version of the album next brings back Gerald Isaac to recapture that spark that made "Your Child" a standout. Over simmering keys and beats, Blige wrestles with the insult behind the injury of betrayal. In the context of this album about finding unity and building peace, "He Think I Don't Know" stands as a dark rumination on the presumption of inequality that wrecks relationships.

A new, playful kind of blues emerges with the following cut, "PMS," cowritten by old friends Terri Robinson (formerly of the Gyrlz) and Tara Tillman. (Al Green also gets writing credit on this, for the sampled strings, as does Chucky Thompson, who produced it, but Thompson is quick to say, "I just stepped back and let the women do what they wanted to do there.") The dry humor that lies behind naming a song "PMS" makes this record a benchmark in Blige's career.

Not that Blige's music is without any humor, and her interviews and live performances had long shown her as an artist whose self-deprecating laughter carried almost as much meaning as any song. But part of what makes Blige so special is that she arrived at a time when music seemed particularly ironic—the cool distance of punk had gone mainstream, gangstas played it bad with a wink to those who "got it," and even country music seemed on the verge of self-parody. Blige's approach was consistently, unabashedly earnest. It's not a stretch to say this seriousness is what announced she was a "queen" when nearly all of the divas of her generation seemed more girlish. And it's worth noting that Blige doesn't play "PMS" for laughs. Still, the humor is inescapable.

"PMS" works on a very basic comic principle—it says out loud what others (at least many women) will recognize but wouldn't likely find a way to say themselves. As her Al Green–like growl details the many reasons for her unreasonableness, over what *New York Daily News* reviewer Dan Aquilante called "her walking-paced acoustic blues," the song grows more than a little comical—even before she gets to lines like "My clothes don't fit/Now, ain't that a bitch?" But as the music broils, she sighs and seethes and cries and yells, and by the time she says, "This is the worst part of everything, the worst part of being a woman," Blige makes it clear the misery is no joke at all.

What's next is an absolute turning point in Blige's career—a break with all that's come before and a commitment to something new.

It's hard to get much bolder and more melodramatic than "Nadia's Theme," the theme to the soap opera *The Young and the Restless*, and "No More Drama" starts with a vinyl record of that song—pops and all—playing to obvious sentimental effect. Blige hums over this record she's playing, and her spoken word voice echoes through the mix, telling listeners she's "so tired." It could be an audio montage advertising the soap opera itself, until the beats kick in.

Blige's voice ties the beats to that soap theme being insistently banged out on piano. By the time she sings "I was young and restless" as an explanation for her tendency to get herself in trouble, she's broken with any sentimentality inherent in those minorkeyed piano chords. This is a song about beating down the melodrama the music represents.

The rhythm grows more insistent, chimes, harp, keys, and strings swirling around the hip hop groove. Blige's declarations that this pain is behind her counterbalance an almost angelic choir of backing vocals. The "Nadia's Theme" chords continue to play, creating a sort of spiraling groove, going in circles that contain such nostalgic grief that it seems they could carry the singer away. At the same time, Blige's vocals sound like those of a woman fighting her way up and out of the current. It's the determination in her voice that gives you hope she'll win, that strength in her voice and the steady call of those backing vocals.

But it's the bridge that convinces. She hangs onto one of her calls for "no more," and a keyboard glissando leads to strong ascending bass and those backing vocalists reassuring her that the drama is indeed behind her. Now she's shouting and growling and testifying with such intensity that only a fool would bet against her. When the song returns to those unadorned "Nadia's Theme" chords, they've been redefined. If only for the moment, she seems at peace, and the chords don't seem to hold the same downward pull. Two chords up and down; they're just holding steady.

Both versions of the album maintain the next progression.

"Where I've Been," a strutting hip hop testimonial that features a rap by Eve, is most noteworthy as the moment Blige talks of the childhood incident that led to her facial scar. She doesn't tell how it happened (she says she never will), but she brings it up in the spirit of rapper Rakim's most famous notion, "It's not where you're from, it's where you're at." She declares that, today, that childhood scar makes her all the more beautiful.

The dappled keyboard lighting of "Beautiful Day" echoes those Roy Ayers compositions Blige references again and again, reminding herself to love the sunshine. The Caribbean-flavored rhythms of "Dance for Me" offer an eye-to-eye celebration of our ability to make music together, just sharing the dance floor, guest star Common calling on "the ghost of Marvin" to help us get it on. These three songs offer thanks for the moment's potential.

"Flying Away" kicks off the final five tracks, all intact from one release to the other. "Flying" uses playful bass and keys to return to the theme of "Steal Away," except this time the dream is transcendence, setting up a movement toward the overtly spiritual.

"2U" prays over the good luck in the previous song, "Never Been," with Houston native Montina Cooper filling in for a gospel choir. Terri Robinson's "In the Meantime" uses serpentine jazz hooks to contemplate how to weather times of doubt—the answer coming down to faith in love itself.

The album closes with a pairing yet again remarkable for its break with what Blige had done before. On the unaccompanied spoken word "Forever No More," Blige shows herself to be a very capable slam poet. Starting off, "No more speechless," she asserts herself as a writer. Having written the majority of the material over the course of her five studio albums, this is nothing new, in one sense, but her words unadorned make their own case. She sums up a series of failed romances unforgettably—"No more relentless sifting through bodies seeking self/Settling through competitive combat for what's left on the shelf."

On one level, she's announcing a renewed faith in God to carry her someplace new. In that sense, "Forever No More" serves as simply an introduction for "Testimony," an unassuming R&B

number that's most remarkable for the fact that it's Blige's first song (give or take "My Life") unequivocally about the role of God in her life, even quoting the nineteenth-century hymn "Blessed Assurance" in the build. This direct spirituality will come back stronger on Blige's next album, *Love & Life*.

---

Though *No More Drama* was an unequivocal success, it took a while to gain its stature. Blige's first single, the Dr. Dre–produced "Family Affair," became her first number-one single in July 2001, and it stayed in that position for six weeks. But the second single, "No More Drama," took almost three months to climb into the pop charts, and the album initially sold little more than *Mary* did. A second version of the album—with a new cover, new tracks, and new guest appearances by Ja Rule and Sean Combs—was released in January, just five months after the album's initial release. It went on to sell another million.

# 16

# Love & Life

*No More Drama*'s release came two days after Blige's musical kid sister, Aaliyah, died in an overloaded plane on a video shoot in the Bahamas. Within two weeks of the album's release, two commercial airlines would crash into the World Trade Center and plunge the United States into a new era dubbed the War on Terror, which would lead to two very real, unending wars in Afghanistan and Iraq. As America plunged headlong into this retaliatory action in Afghanistan, Blige's image crying "no more" in the video spoke for the many Americans whose lives would soon be turned upside down by the upcoming wars as well as the many thousands who protested the rush to war.

In February, though her single wasn't nominated for an award, "No More Drama" had struck such a chord that Mary J. Blige was invited to perform at the Grammys. Wearing gold pants and jacket, with golden spiked hair, Blige started the song as a direct testimonial to the audience, like she was simply telling them what she wanted. By midway through, she was filled with the spirit— high stepping across the apron, stooping and waving and moving the crowd with an intensity altogether rare at the industry award ceremony. She ended by crying out Fannie Lou Hamer's line, "I'm sick and tired of being sick and tired," then adding, "I'm sick and tired of being deprived of the things I've worked so hard for." The crowd exploded with applause.

But the losses kept coming. Almost simultaneous with the launch of her *No More Drama* tour, Blige's close peers on the pop charts TLC lost the group's dynamic rapper, Lisa "Left Eye" Lopes, killed in a car accident while vacationing in Honduras. A beautiful picture of Blige clutching Lopes tight circulates the Internet. Blige looks every bit the eight inches taller she is, and she looks as happy to hold Lopes as Lopes looks happy to be held. The two no doubt felt some connection. Lopes was by far the most outspoken member of TLC, and she and Blige both had famously dramatic personal lives—Lopes gaining infamy by burning down (accidentally, but . . .) the mansion she shared with Atlanta Falcons wide receiver Andre Rison. Lopes's death gave resonance to the themes of *No More Drama* Blige never could have intended.

Despite all of this loss, the album she began at the end of the *No More Drama* tour exemplified a newfound joy suggested by its title, *Love & Life*. Released in August 2003, the album's cover shows Blige looking remarkably healthy, strong, and (it's irresistible to point out) sexy. It's cliché, but it's also true that Blige looks like a woman in love, and in fact she was. She'd first started dating her future husband and manager, Kendu Isaacs, about the time she started working on *No More Drama*. The couple married in December after the album's release, and *Love & Life* seems to capture the relationship in full blossom.

The cover all but illustrates the point. Blige had always been pretty, but she'd lost some of the modesty about her body she'd had in the past. In 2004, she told *W*'s Jancee Dunn that Isaacs had a lot to do with that cover. The couple talked back and forth during the interview, Blige stating that Isaacs told her she needed a sexy cover, "Because it's not only girls buying your album. . . . Men want to put that album cover on the wall."

As giddy in love as she may have been, Blige was making serious business and artistic decisions based upon the newfound stability in her relationship. Since leaving Sean Combs, she'd increasingly worked with her sister LaTonya as a comanager, but now she gave that job to Isaacs and reunited with Combs. Upon the album's release, she explained to *Jet*, "After you say something like 'no more drama' . . . you continue to work on not having drama and the way you work on that is you fall in love with yourself. I don't mean that vainly. I mean get yourself a foundation." On one level, that's what makes this album art shine—whether in the sporty jacket and T-shirt on the cover or wearing black fur inside—Blige looks happy being herself, and that's striking because it is indeed new.

And *Love & Life* is a very new kind of record. Unlike Blige's previous albums, *Love & Life* avoids set pieces that sound like a Stevie Wonder or Diana Ross record. Everything here sounds slimmed down, snug against the beat. There are no big pop moments either, very few sugary hooks. This is an adult R&B record as seemingly unconcerned with broad-base commercial appeal as anything Blige had made to date.

---

At this point in his career, he'd become P. Diddy, but to Blige, he's always Puff, and that's what Blige calls him when she answers the phone at the start of her sixth studio album, 2003's *Love & Life*—after three albums apart, a reunion. On the first album, Combs was a frustrated manager, calling his protégée "nigga" and "man" and telling her he knows she's there and she better pick up the phone. On the second album, he threw in a "baby," but he still called her "nigga" and said, "Be on time, man." This time, he calls her "Mary" and asks her if she's ready. She answers, "I'm always ready."

What follows is yet another introduction, by the reigning king of rap, Jay-Z, on the eve of his "retirement" release, *The Black Album* (a nonretirement if ever there was one, but noteworthy because Jay-Z's first career arc ran its course between *My Life* and this career height for Blige). With the Def Jam recording artist at her side, Blige asserts she isn't alone while paying this visit to Combs. She is an independent artist working with the biggest names in the business. At the end of the intro, Combs pays tribute to her, affirming, eleven years down the line, there's "only one Queen of Hip Hop Soul."

"Don't Go" opens the story with woodwinds and harp, Blige's vibrato in the background wordlessly forecasting the chord changes. Scene: woodland at sunrise, birds calling in the mist. Her voice comes closer as the beat rises.

"Every day is not a perfect day for you and I," she sings, on yet another cut penned with her brother. In this case, with a romping, staggered beat that obliterates that pastoral setting, Blige sings of real love as something messy. As the title proclaims, she's calling to her lover, "Don't go," arguing these rough days are to be expected.

The first song that sounds like a single on this record is "Not Today." As if she knows its importance for her audience but wants to separate it from the core ideas on the album, Blige introduces the song as "another one of those 'Heartbreak Hotel' joints for the ladies." Pizzicato strings scale up and down, hinting at "No More Drama," over a fat bass and drums with taunting En Vogue–like backing vocals. Eve plays center stage here, taking the lying lover out with her rhymes. Blige seems content to be a supporting character in this old drama. Her mind is elsewhere.

On "Finally Made It (Interlude)," Blige returns to spoken word. Against all of the losses she's suffered, she feels "spiritually successful," and she tells her fans she's "striving" for a "perfection" she never dreamed she could have. She says, "If I can do it, I know you all can do it too," and though it's a noble sentiment, this is the first time in her career when Blige doesn't seem to be using the contradictions with much precision. This isn't the slam poetry of "Forever No More," unfortunately, because that disciplined phrasing might better have served her purpose. Though she clearly wrote the lyrics, this sounds more like Combs's familiar media posturing rather than the kind of insight typical of Blige.

Such contradictions are easy enough to dismiss once "Ooh!"'s hooks kick in. Backing vocalists Kandace Love and Shannon Jones spin joy-filled confections out of the sexy refrain. "I can't shake this thing/It's the sweetest pain," Blige sings with an ecstatic urgency blurring the line between sexuality, spirituality, and addiction.

By the end of this popping mix of horn and jangling percussion, sounding at times a little like Al Green at the height of ecstasy, she's erased any such line.

With the arrival of 50 Cent on "Let Me Be the 1" and then Method Man on the Dr. Dre cut that served as the first single, "Love @ 1st Sight," Blige forcefully asserts that, though she may be singing about being happy, she's still grounded in the tough streets that raised her. The video for this single shows Blige sitting on a stoop with Method Man and dancing in the streets as she had in her early videos—granted these now look like Hollywood back-lot streets rather than the high-rise projects in their original video together.

The spoken-versed "Free" carries the album's central theme further—freedom from mental slavery, "being my own worst enemy." Gently lifting keys and smooth backing vocals suggest the ability to rise can be as easy as letting go of all that drags you down. But Blige keeps the contradictions on the table, a small dangerous voice admitting, "I might give out."

Sung against chimes sounding alarm, "Friends" calls up another R&B theme tackled in hit singles by Jody Watley and TLC, the inability to trust self-proclaimed allies. As this song ends, Blige states, "Give me another track immediately," and launches into "Press On," which opens with the great line, "Life has a way of making you live it." By this cut, three songs deep into celebrity troubles, it might seem Blige would be at risk of losing her audience, but her strength is in finding the universal in her specifics. Everyone has to fight to be free of their demons, everyone has experienced personal treachery, and everyone knows the contradictions in this song. Some part of everyone's life is always going wrong, some part of what we do will go unappreciated, and some part of us has to always be on guard. Singing of her determination to keep going, Blige turns one personal mantra after another into an anthem for women struggling everywhere.

While she distances herself from the breakup songs on this record, they clearly serve as statements of strength. "It's a Wrap" sets up the album's third interlude, "Message in Our Music," a nod to the O'Jays song of the same name interwoven with music she'd used in concert for some time, Kool & the Gang's "Summer Madness." With layered, whispery vocals, Blige calls on her listeners to let the music make them feel "you can really touch the sky." That stance, that position of strength, is the message itself.

The close of this album focuses on sexuality and spirituality. "All My Love" takes a piece of the Addrisi Brothers' "Never My Love" and builds a confectionary valentine dedicated to giving one's self over to another. When Blige begins to push the boundaries of the frothy track with agile cries of ecstasy, it takes an oblique turn toward gospel.

Over acoustic guitar, Blige sings against her own backing vocals on "Ultimate Relationship (A.M.)," a love song to God. It's a bold moment in a couple of ways—first, because it's the most explicitly religious song since "Testimony," even more so invoking the name of Jesus. There's also the unshakeable sensuality of this morning rendezvous. If soul music started as gospel music turned toward sex, Blige seems to have reversed that dynamic here, saving the line "nothing like the way you make me feel" for these moments alone with divinity.

---

Like *No More Drama*, *Love & Life* debuted at number one on the *Billboard* album chart, but it sold about a third fewer copies, "Love @ 1st Sight" and "Ooh!" being the only singles to crack the Top Forty, the Method Man single the only one to make it to the R&B Top Ten. Blige no doubt knew she was taking a risk with *Love & Life*, but she was likely unprepared for a roller-coaster ride from career highs to career lows.

She seems to have a sense she's in some trouble with the record in an October 2003 interview with *Ebony*'s Kevin Chappell. Chappell questions whether her focus on happiness is as relatable for her audience as her past suffering. He writes:

But it's that chance, and the utter idea that people actually prefer a scorned Mary to a proud one, and the whole notion of her life being only as good as it is bad that, in mid-sentence, and without warning, becomes too disconcerting for her to fathom. "You know, I really don't care about those people who say that I'm too happy, because it's obvious that they don't care about me," she says, as she doubles over and curls into a weeping ball of confusion, breaking down as tears stream along her cheeks and she clutches her face between her hands. . . . "They think this is entertainment. This Mary J. Blige thing is not entertainment. . . . They don't have to buy one of my records. Don't. Somebody else in this world wants to be happy. If it's 10 people, then fine."

She regains composure and begins to talk about why she's proud of the new record. "It consists of a lot of things I have in my life right now, which is love and confidence and strength. Understanding that I am a spirit, and that it has nothing to do with religion but knowing exactly who I am. . . . For me to even be able to express myself to that level of understanding, I'm very proud of *Love & Life*. Vocally, I'm proud of it. Lyrically, I'm proud of it. Concept-wise, I'm proud of it."

And listening to *Love & Life*, it's clear she should be proud. You can look long and hard before you find such a unified record, both sonically and thematically—all of its hip hop effects tightly wound around a funky beat thrown like a lifeline. Unfortunately, the lack of vulnerability and imperfection—traits that had always been key to Blige's artistry—apparent on this record left that line difficult to catch for even her most devoted listeners.

And it's no wonder. Blige was beginning the second decade of her career by launching into all-but-uncharted territory in popular music—adulthood and commitment. How does one write about marriage with the same vitality as romance? How does one write about stability at the cost of drama? How does one sell joy as convincingly, as infectiously, as pain? Few pop musicians have dared to address these questions. In some ways, Blige was just getting started.

# 17

# Live from Los Angeles

I find myself sifting among very different memories for comparisons to the live Mary J. Blige experience. I think of the crowd excitement defined best by James Brown and inhabited later by Prince and Janelle Monáe. I think of Janet Jackson's amazing *Rhythm Nation 1814* tour, which brought the same level of intensity to R&B. However, if I let go of genre distinctions, I most frequently go to Bruce Springsteen, who has a similar sense of artist and audience in a journey taken together; who, like Blige, uses the shape of the show like a complex story arc; and who, like Blige, leaves me feeling I've left my body and been renewed by the process. That last quality certainly comes out of the philosophy of concert as tent meeting—all of these qualities can be tied to American popular music's church roots.

For Blige, those roots run deep, and she rarely takes the stage anywhere without transforming that space, even if only momentarily, into something sacred. For these reasons, it is hard to overstate the historical significance of Blige's decision, at the end of the *Love & Life* tour, to release two live shows on DVD: *An Intimate Evening with Mary J. Blige*, recorded at the House of Blues the night before the February 8, 2004, Grammy broadcast, and *Live from Los Angeles*, a concert film shot at the Universal Amphitheatre May 8, 2004.

The House of Blues show is certainly worth watching. It has some of the high points of the Amphitheatre show, as well as guest appearances by Elton John on "Deep Inside" and "I Guess That's Why They Call It the Blues" and Sting on his duet with Blige, "Whenever I Say Your Name," which won a Grammy that same year. But *Live from Los Angeles* deserves recognition alongside classic live sets like James Brown's *Live at the Apollo*, Otis Redding's *Live in Europe*, and, still the greatest hip hop live album, Boogie Down Productions' *Live Hardcore Worldwide*.

First, the show works beautifully as a retrospective—starting with the early singles and working its way to a coherent statement of how this music fits into the *Love & Life* vision. It's also an exciting piece of theater—relaying the songs as a version of the Mary J. Blige story. Finally, it's Blige using her gospel upbringing to push the core songs in her catalog to a place beyond what may even be possible on a record. The show is tightly choreographed from beginning to end, but Blige manages to improvise so often and with such intensity that the video record all but casts Pentecostal fire into your living room.

If you have any doubt about how much control a hip hop diva like Blige may have over her theatrical appearances, the DVD extras are particularly interesting. Her backup singers—Kemba Francis, Tiffany Palmer, Karen Bernod, and Carlos Ricketts Jr.— testify about how her energy level pushes them to do their best. Her guitarist, Shonn Hinton, tells how patient she was with him and how it put him at ease that she was there to make it work with him. You see Blige, without makeup, breaking down each number and talking in detail with each band member about when to push, when to pull back, and when to keep doing what they're doing. It's clearly her show. Even manager/husband Isaacs seems to quietly wait for her to call the shots.

That May night in 2004, Blige commanded the stage from the moment she took it. She sometimes looked vulnerable, having to keep her breath to sing and sometimes hitting a momentary harsh note while stepping in and out of the dancers' choreography, but that meant nothing. Few artists have had a stronger presence in the spotlight. Despite six backup dancers actually growing up behind her—changing from schoolgirl and B-boy costumes to adult couples in black suits and white dresses—Blige, dressed in plain gray cotton, kept the focus through a five-song medley of early hits, except when she directed it elsewhere. At one point, during "Real Love," she turned sideways and looked up at the screen behind her. On the video screens, which had been showing various magazine pictures from Blige's career, a portrait of Christopher Wallace held the frame while the deejay played his rap from that early hit's remix—"Look up in the sky! Is it a bird? Is it a plane? No, it's Mary Jane."

At the ten-minute mark, the medley finished and Blige slowed things down, doing full versions of three songs about believing in one's self. A table came out, with a waiter. She was soon seated for a breakup scene, singing "My Love." She closed the set, donning a white fedora, the dancers in black fedoras, with "I Can Love You"—again deferring to a video screen. This time it was Lil' Kim doing her rap from the song's video. On the screen, the way the two tough New York girls played off each other—Blige gesturing to illustrate Kim's points, the two dancing together—was a powerful statement of sisterhood, even when trying to hold its own against what was happening on stage.

It was after this statement of women's self-worth that Blige left the stage and the band showed its chops with hard blasts of keyboard and bass fueling a conga break, a drum solo, and, finally, Shonn Hinton's guitar carrying the instrumental excitement to heights well beyond the fireworks on the video screen or the theater pyrotechnics. The interlude continued with "Message in Our Music," the backup singers taking all of the vocals. When Blige reemerged dressed in blue cotton similar to the gray she had on before, a very good concert became great.

The first big moment came when the video screens filled with images of children playing around city projects, Blige's voice scatting in the background. The band kicked into Philip Bailey's 1984 album cut "Children of the Ghetto" as Blige walked out and took a seat in a chair surrounded by candles. She sang the song as if talking directly from her own experience, pumping her bicep on the line "toughness is our motto." Hinton's guitar burned behind her vocals, while the rest of the band maintained a restrained cool until the second refrain, when Blige sang "Keep your head to the sky," and she allowed that guitar to lift her up off of her seat.

She began to improvise over the groove, singing "na na na" between fast drumbeats, while waving her free arm, shouting "hold on tight" over and over again. Stooped, looking at the floor, she cried, "Mommy might not love you," and "Daddy might not want you."

But she began pointing at the sky again and jumping up and down. And she cried out again, as a confession and as a statement of solidarity—"I am I am I am a child of the ghetto too."

She then began to testify. "Every single day I have a problem trying to keep my head up . . . every day . . . but let me tell you something . . . people, I've got no choice! I've come too far to put my head down. You all are here, so I got to keep my head up. You're here!

"Thank you so much. I keep my head up for everybody out there that can't, and every time you look around and see Mary J. Blige with my head up, you put your head up. It ain't easy, it ain't easy," she admitted, finally finding the stance she'd needed in her *Love & Life* spoken word.

She used this to transition into "My Life," sung over a backdrop of childhood and career photographs. She bolstered her connection to the crowd by giving them the mic for the line "Say what's on your mind," and she scatted and she testified, adding lines like "Love is an action word," underlining the debt she was trying to repay to her fans. "I gotta keep moving," she said in closing, so "keep on moving, y'all . . . don't let 'em stop you."

Then, with, "Ladies, ladies, it is our turn," she began the now staple heart-to-heart with the women in the crowd. "Why are so many children being abandoned and left alone?" she asked. "So let's talk about these babies, let's talk about the babies and why," she added, before launching into "Your Child," singing to her fans from the stage apron.

You could hear the women in the audience singing along as she called out, "Girlfriend, she wasn't disrespectful," pointing into the crowd as she told this story of two women who come together over a child the man they have in common is trying to ignore. At one point, Blige rocked an imaginary baby as she sang. Soon after, she threw away the script, taking this deep into her own history and crying out to her own father, "How could you do this to me?" repeating the question "why," repeating the thought, "I didn't ask to come here."

Then she began to talk to the men. "Fathers, please go see your little girl. . . . Go get her and tell her she's somebody. . . . Something's wrong when Daddy's not there." She said her own missing father contributed to her becoming "a drug-induced, alcoholic whore, looking for a father, looking for somebody to say they love me." She repeated to the men that they needed to see their little girls, to tell them, "You're beautiful," shouted down at an imaginary child standing beside her, "You are everything."

"This is what's bothering me every day," she said in summation, telling the women, "He don't love you, and guess who he don't love the most? Himself. So, brothers, I understand what happened to you too." At this point, she had taken this secular theme all the way to church.

With this she transitioned to "The Love I Never Had," the song sounding more gospel than ever, bass and drums building around the call to "Wake up!" As this refrain returned, Blige hunched her shoulders and began jumping up and down around the stage. She was feeling the spirit now, no longer wallowing in the pain, and she began a scat version of a guitar battle, trading vocal lines with guitarist Hinton, singing her own version of the guitar leads and watching close for what the guitarist would do next. They ended this song leaning on each other back-to-back, rock and roll stars.

A powerful "Not Gon' Cry" followed, the crowd singing along like before. But when it was over, she said, "Get the dirt off your shoulder," flicking her shoulders, and launched into "It's a Wrap" from *Love & Life*. In this move, she swept weakness into strength, getting happy in a stooped church dance before she left the stage again, and her backing singers sang the title "love and life." Blige appeared in silhouette on the screens above, dancing open-armed to "Free (Interlude)."

Thunder crashed, the piano chords to "No More Drama" began, and Blige returned to the stage again, dressed in white hip-huggers and a matching white jacket over a black shirt. She sang the song as fog billowed at her feet and images of the sky filled the screens. Once she got through the initial verses, she gave it everything she had. She ran back and forth across the stage, she leapfrogged, and she screamed, the song's sands-through-the-hourglass chords warning that time wasn't on her side. She closed singing, "I'm so sick and tired of being sick and tired," before stating, "The enemy was me," and she shouted it again, "Me." And she shouted it one more time, "Me."

"I hated me, and that was the problem," she declared, closing the climactic exorcism and moving to the final celebrations that would close the show. She'd dropped the white jacket to dance with the girls on her year's big single, "Love @ 1st Sight," and then she dedicated "Everything" to her fans, stating, "Without you there is absolutely nothing for Mary J. Blige." During that song, she made it clear she was serious about the literal meaning, pledging to treat her audience "like kings and queens."

At the end of the set, she gave a couple of fans gifts and held one girl's arm as she told the crowd, "I didn't have a high school education, and I couldn't get a real job, but you went and bought the *What's the 411?* album, and you went and bought the *My Life* album, and you went and bought . . ." listing each of her albums. She closed stating, "Thank you. You gave me a reason to live. Thank you," and she left the stage.

After the crowd called her back out, chanting, "Mary, Mary,

Mary . . ." she returned for the expected "Family Affair," an excuse to dance with her fans as much as anything. Red, white, and blue confetti blasted out over the stage and the crowd. Blige slipped away again, the show ending with the band playing an extended outro and each dancer breaking for the crowd.

*I listen to Mary for her conviction and honesty; her voice is secondary to the emotion she conveys in her raw portrayal of life.*

**Natasha Ria El-Scari, poet, Cave Canem Fellow (2014 interview with the author)**

# 18

# Message in Our Music

"Everybody should look at Katrina," Mary J. Blige told the *Guardian* journalist Zoe Williams in late 2005. "Don't act like it can't happen to us. That's how it's been for years. . . . I haven't seen anything change. I've just seen things get worse. We would have been those people in New Orleans, the people who couldn't get out, the people who died."

In her interviews in the months after 2005's Hurricane Katrina, Blige seemed willing to talk publicly about issues in a way she'd rarely done before. All of America (and the world) watched while New Orleans residents crowded into the Superdome (twenty-six thousand in an emergency facility set up for a few hundred) and waited on rooftops for help. Four days of horror passed as nothing substantial happened to rescue the sixty thousand black and poor residents of neighborhoods like the city's Lower Ninth Ward, many living in the top floors and on the roofs of flooded homes.

Fifty levees had failed Monday, August 29. But it was Friday, September 2, before any large-scale rescue began. That day, President Bush toured the area, and, that same day, concerned about looting, Louisiana governor Kathleen Blanco gave shoot-to-kill orders.

Certainly many black viewers of that Friday's NBC benefit, *A Concert for Hurricane Relief*, understood what motivated Kanye West's now famous outburst. After Mike Myers delivered a scripted statement about three levee breaches and five feet of water filling homes, West took his turn and went off script.

Nervously but deliberately, he stared into the camera and said, "I hate the way they portray us in the media. You see a black family, it says, 'They're looting.' You see a white family, it says, 'They're looking for food.' And, you know, it's been five days because most of the people are black."

Standing next to West, Mike Myers looked nervously back and forth at the monitor, uncertain when to come in again. West continued, chastising himself for not acting sooner but pledging to take action immediately, adding, "So anybody out there that wants to do anything that we can help. . . . America is set up to help the poor, the black people, the less well-off, as slow as possible.

"I mean, the Red Cross is doing everything they can. We already realize a lot of people that could help are at war right now, fighting another way—and they've given them permission to go down and shoot us!"

A seemingly rattled Myers took the moment to deliver the next part of his scripted speech before West delivered his most famous line—"George Bush doesn't care about black people."

The camera cut away to a startled Chris Tucker, who transitioned elsewhere, but West's point had been heard 'round the world. Blige certainly grasped West's desperate need to make this statement at this moment, with so many lives so clearly at stake.

In Blige's interview with Williams, she seemed emboldened to talk about the impact of race on her career. "The blacker you are, the worse it is for you. If you're mixed, you've got a shot. If you cater to what white America wants you to do and how they want you to look, you can survive. But if you want to be yourself, and try to do things that fit you, and your skin, nobody cares about that. At the end of the day, white America dominates and rules. And it's racist."

West's words just seven days before certainly echoed through Blige's duet with the Irish rock band U2 for yet another hurricane relief telecast, *Shelter from the Storm: A Concert for the Gulf Coast*, an all-star benefit put together by Joel Gallen, who had all but created the form with the 9/11 benefit *America: A Tribute to Heroes*. Blige was also being courted to play Nina Simone for a new movie, and Blige had read Simone's autobiography earlier that year. Her relationship with Simone and a lifetime of thought went into her performance of that song, race playing no small part.

Blige's history with "One" extended back a couple of years before any of this. Interscope's Jimmy Iovine suggested she perform the song at the 2003 MusiCares Person of the Year tribute to U2's lead singer and songwriter, Bono. She loved the song and impressed guitarist Shane Fontayne (of Lone Justice) so much that he wrote in his February 2003 blog: "We were running a little behind schedule . . . and Mary J. Blige had been observing things for a while. She came up and sang 'One' appropriately just once, giving everything to the lone performance. And 'everything' in this regard was a performance that was so emotional I knew as soon as it was done that we wouldn't see her again until the following night. She was shaking as she left the stage. There was no point in 'rehearsing' it any more." The next day at MusiCares, she reportedly left everyone else shaking.

In 2006, Blige told Gavin Martin,

> As I learned the song, when I was listening to the words, they struck, they got in my spirit, and they really made me think of everything in the world because you know the World Trade Center, New York was blowing up, and it was just crazy and it just really got to my heart, the song, I love it. The music was incredible, Bono was singing the mess out of it, and that's when I fell in love with that record.
>
> Let's fast forward to a year after that. I'm sitting around with the president of the record company, Jimmy Iovine, and we're sitting in his house and the song comes on. And I get that same feeling again, like I have to record this song. I said that to Jimmy, and Jimmy said to me, "Don't you forget that you said that." And I said, "I won't."

So when I went in the studio to record my album, which was a year later, Jimmy reminded me that I wanted to record the record. So, it ended up on the album.

Martin asked her what it was about the lyrics of the song that attracted her.

With great emphasis, she recited,

"Love is a temple/Love is a higher law/You ask for me to enter/ But then you make me crawl/I can't keep holding on to what you got."

That right there? . . . is so powerful to me. "Love *is* the temple; love *is* a higher law. You ask for me to enter," meaning people use love, they lure people with so-called love, and then when they get in it, they got to go through so much and call it love just like the way we live here on this earth, like, this place, the United States say they care about us and stuff like that, and we got to go through so much. There's so many people who don't have. Those people are crawling. So many people with AIDS, so many people dying; we live in the land of the free and the home of the brave, but it's hurtful to watch some of the stuff that goes on. A lot of us are fortunate because we're working hard, but in this system we're still faced with racism and segregation and separation. But at the end of the day it was those lyrics that were really, really strong to me, that made me think of everybody and how we're in this all together.

"What is your experience of racism being in the record industry?" Martin asked. Blige responded,

Uhm, just the fact that, you know, sometimes I can't . . . they don't want me on shows or they don't want me in places, and they'll say I'm too urban, like my music is too urban for this pop station or whatever the case may be, unless I actually make a record that is suitable for their ears and feels good to them. If I give them like an *urban* urban record, they won't play it.

It just all looks weird to me, like . . . what kind of record do I need to make? This is what I am and this is who I am, so this is the kind of stuff that is going to come out of me.

Of course, Blige's blackness was a significant part of what excited both Jimmy Iovine and Bono about Blige singing the MusiCares benefit. Before she came out that night in 2003, Bono made his excitement known—"Mary J. Blige is going to sing 'One' for God's sake! We're going to church this evening whether we like it or not!"

But Blige brought something more to her cover of "One," which most of the world first encountered on the night of the *Shelter from the Storm* benefit two years later. Church was in there, as it is in everything Blige does, but this service was clearly about matters of class and race and gender.

That September night in 2005, the power of that first recorded performance of the duet remains palpable. U2 started what may be its most beautiful song with appropriate solemnity—camera on guitar, snare and keys gently ringing out. Bono stepped to the mic, and almost whispered the question, "Is it getting better?" He sang that verse solidly but seemingly shaken, almost frail. At the end of the refrain, he called out, "Mary?"

With a black wide-brimmed fedora stating volumes next to Bono's white cowboy hat, Blige stepped out of the red-and-black background and took her place by Bono's side, asking, "Did I disappoint you?"

Immediately, the song's central argument became evident. She pointed her finger, singing, "We're one, but we're not the same." When Blige and Bono doubled their voices on the wordless refrain that followed, the contrast between his sweet open notes and her soulful vibrato drove the point home.

When Blige took the next verse, she confronted all the white hats who had taken offense at Kanye West, who had blamed the victims, who continued trying to rationalize away the racism of this national tragedy. "You gave me nothing, now that's all I got," she cried.

"We hurt each other, then we do it again," she shouted, before pointing again. And that's when she sang those lines about being asked to crawl and no longer being able to hold on to what you got. In those soaring vocals, she sang with enough fury to overturn anything in her path.

When the camera panned back to Bono, he looked close to tears. She shouted out to her sisters, and splayed her fingers in a gesture of laying hands as she hung on to the call to her brothers.

When they reached the call to "carry each other, carry each other," she was rocking her arm back and forth the way she'd rocked an imaginary baby in other shows, but this was a move toward the audience, like the tossing of a ball.

In her 2008 essay, "All That You Can't Leave Behind: Black Female Soul Singing and the Politics of Surrogation in the Age of Catastrophe," Princeton professor Daphne A. Brooks wrote, "Blige's *Shelter from the Storm* version of U2's 'One' is perhaps the most insurgent political work of a black female pop singer since Nina Simone's 'Four Women' and 'Mississippi Goddamn,'" and Brooks made the case to prove it. She closed with the succinct summation, "Blige recycles 'One'—a song that mainlines the twice-removed blues of the Mississippi Delta by way of Keith Richards and the Edge—replacing it and replaying it as the soundtrack of the Louisiana Gulf Coast women who, in this moment in time, on this night, at this benefit, will—through this act of soulful surrogation—indeed have their say."

Brooks's argument is a richly layered comparison of Beyoncé's and Blige's work during this Gulf Coast disaster. What's noteworthy for our purposes is that Blige wasn't done having her say with "One" after this Katrina performance. When she finally recorded it on *The Breakthrough*, she would prove that she was prepared to follow through on the implications.

# 19

# The Breakthrough

Despite the flagging sales for *Love & Life*, Blige maintained a high profile throughout 2004 and 2005. She was featured in a *60 Minutes* segment, performed for various award shows, guested in Wyclef Jean's All Star Jam at Carnegie Hall, released the *Live from Los Angeles* and *An Intimate Evening with Mary J. Blige* DVDs, and joined friends Eric Clapton and Elton John for a fund-raiser to address the Indian Ocean tsunami.

She noticeably reached for new audiences. At another fund-raiser for Katrina, the Condé Nast Fashion Rocks concert, Blige performed a stunning cover of Jerry Ragovoy and Bert Berns's "Piece of My Heart," a song all but owned by Janis Joplin. For those six minutes on the stage of Radio City Music Hall, Blige made it hers.

Blige paid tribute, as she always pays tribute, to the Joplin classic, but she also used it to assert her connection to rock history. After rock guitarist Dave Navarro introduced her, Blige appeared on a riser wearing a white floppy hat over a bell-bottomed white suit. Her band's forceful take on Big Brother and the Holding Company swelled, and Blige tossed her hat to the side and strutted down to center stage.

From the start, the capacity crowd writhed with excitement and shouted for joy, but Blige kept kicking things up a notch. She was soon banging a tambourine over Shonn Hinton's guitar solo, then standing back-to-back with him in another rock tableau. Before the final build, she started talking to the ladies in the audience about the need for the man to "take the whole thing."

That's when she took off. Against a swirling rock crescendo, she shouted, "Take it, take it, take it"—fifteen times—her eyes widening and her legs bending to punctuate each point. The entire crowd took to a standing ovation as she sang that final "if it makes you feel good," Blige waving with her fingers and ending with a triumphant kick.

She seemed well suited to the role when *Vibe* gave her a Legends award in November. However, even though she accepted it graciously when Quincy Jones and Jimmy Iovine handed it to her, she soon cracked, "I know you gotta be like sixty to get a Legends award." Before leaving the stage, she congratulated Mariah Carey on the three awards—R&B voice of the year, artist of the year, and album of the year—Blige's peer had won that night. Carey's career had started four years before Blige's (Blige has recalled singing along with Carey's first single as a teenager, straining to hit the notes), and Carey's new album, *The Emancipation of Mimi*, dominated the radio most of 2005. With her own new album set to come out, Blige didn't want to be a "legend"; she wanted the kind of year Carey was having.

Released in December of 2005, *The Breakthrough*, Mary J. Blige's seventh studio album, moved her artistic vision forward. Like *Love & Life*, it was a record about newfound peace and commitment, but it honored the fight involved in maintaining such gains.

It asserted a renewed independence from Combs, but Blige's new concept of individuality was tied up with a need for social connection. While it's understandable that more than one critic agreed with the *Guardian*'s Caroline Sullivan, calling the album "a love letter to [Mary's] husband," *The Breakthrough* was no more a Valentine's Day card than its closing song, "One"—with lines like

"Have you come here to play Jesus to the lepers in your head?"—was a simple affirmation of racial togetherness.

---

A decade later, *The Breakthrough* still sounds a fresh call for love and community. On the opener, "No One Will Do"—a rousing mix of the O'Jays, huge hip hop beats and voices coming from every direction—Blige certainly hands her husband that valentine, seeking to ease his mind, but she also calls it an "SOS," a cry for help, forecasting the contradiction that runs throughout the album. Mary J. Blige no longer wants to stick to the blues. She tackles themes from a position of strength, and she sings songs of praise more often than songs of woe. Though this stance cost *Love & Life* some dramatic tension, *The Breakthrough* finds tensions aplenty in the workings of relationships.

Not that every relationship here works; she still learns by revisiting points of no return. Rodney Jerkins's dazzling production on "Enough Cryin"—wall-shaking beats framing ricocheted keyboard effects, crystal clear keyboard figures, hand-held shakers, and sweeping strings—comes from the perspective of a woman slamming the door on the past. This cut was originally meant to feature Lil' Kim's one-time friend/sometime nemesis, rapper Foxy Brown, to put the smackdown on the man in the song. That decision may well have come from the fact that Lil' Kim was currently serving jail time for a perjury charge, but Brown couldn't do it either, because she suffered serious hearing loss. Blige's fix was to go ahead and do the rhymes herself, creating a rap persona, "Brook Lynn," named for the hometown of both of these MCs. On this cut, the need for others is both the reason for the breakup and the cause for Blige creating a new character to lend her song hip hop support.

Using her recent homework on Nina Simone, Blige plays off a sample of Simone's "Feeling Good" on the next track, "About You." A classically trained jazz artist who all but defied even that much genre labeling, Simone represents an artistic tradition outside of the pop music associated with Blige, and she also represents an explicitly activist tradition. By using this sample on this track produced by celebrated producer will.i.am, Blige established her interest in broadening the possibilities of popular music. The choice of Simone's "Feeling Good" also explored the nature of happiness Blige had been chasing since *No More Drama*.

Simone's 1965 record did amazing things with this theme. The initial tension in that record was that she sang the first refrain a cappella, talking to herself about her sense of a new life. When she sang, "It's a new dawn, it's a new day, it's a new life for me," at first she sounded like she was trying to convince herself of this truth. Despite the taunting sounds of burlesque horns undercutting her optimism, when she sang, "Freedom is mine, and I know how I feel," her voice soared, braced for a struggle you believed she could win.

Blige uses the Simone record to talk to her lover. She reassures him, "You know how I feel," and Simone's vocal echoes those words with decidedly blue notes. This is a song about negotiating boundaries—"I don't wanna be free . . . but sometimes I don't want to be bothered." While Simone's song sounds like an independent woman filling her empty places with a little hope, Blige's version fights for personal space.

"Be without You" tackles the equally necessary fight to maintain relationships, and it struck a resounding chord with a wide audience. Though it didn't chart as high on the Top Forty as "Family Affair" (no. 1) or "Not Gon' Cry" (no. 2), "Be without You" (no. 3), this album's first single, spent fifteen weeks at the top of the Hot R&B/Hip-Hop charts, a record not to be outdone until Robin Thicke's "Blurred Lines" in 2013. It also stayed on the R&B charts for seventy-five weeks, almost a year and a half. Released two months before the album, "Be without You" helped give *The Breakthrough*, at least for the first week, the strongest sales of Blige's career.

But the real breakthrough of "Be without You" is not simply its commercial viability, especially on the new-artist-chasing R&B charts. Simply and directly, it encapsulates the tenets of Blige's twenty-first-century career—the fight for love is the most important struggle between individuals and between communities.

In no small part the musical creation of hot young Atlanta producer Bryan-Michael Cox, who had just delivered Mariah Carey to one of her career's shining moments with "Shake It Off," "Be without You" still sounds contemporary a decade later.

If you were listening to pop radio in 2005 through 2007, you couldn't escape "Be without You." It was one of a handful of records that argued for the artistic integrity of pop radio five decades into the rock and roll era. Like "No More Drama," it's built around a repeated piano figure. But where that earlier hit found its greatness in living up to its ostentatiousness, this record is subtle. Piano cuts a spry groove around a huge bass line. There are other touches here—guitar filling in for the piano, bongos, and tom-toms along with sweeping strings—that keep the mix lively and surprising, but it all revolves around that bold center. Blige sings all of the vocals, which bounce around in the mix, sometimes spoken and sometimes shouted.

She begins with a hushed voice, recalling the romantic origins of her marriage. Then, when she talks of the adversity she and her husband have faced, backing vocals speak "yes," urging her onward. "I've been too strong for too long," she sings on the first chorus, and warm backing vocals affirm her, the intimacy of pillow talk delivered as church testimonial.

The music breaks, allowing the singer to step back and announce, "I've got a question for ya." Now she's facing off with her husband, asking him questions about his integrity only to reassure him that she wouldn't betray him either. Her voice soars into the next build, when she turns the refrain into a statement of solidarity, "We've been too strong for too long!"

Then comes a bridge with cascading backing vocals. She's now talking to the church—telling the men what they need to do for the women, and the women what the men need from them. At the end of the final refrain, her voice is sailing high above the mix, as if the congregation has set her free. That single's mix of secular and spiritual is a primer for Twenty-First-Century Soul 101.

The album then reaches for the hip hop community. The Mohawks' 1968 hit instrumental "The Champ" has had its skipping keyboards and strutting drum track (as well as the shouted title) used in enough rap records to rival James Brown's "Funky Drummer" break. Its prominence throughout "Gonna Breakthrough" ushers alter ego Brook Lynn to appear again, pledging to "ride like the queen I am." A song about artistic commitment, this near-title track is a modest "I'll Take You There" for a soul queen wanting to emphasize the project girl who taught her the way.

That project girl is close on "Good Woman Down" as Blige talks to her "troubled sisters." She rationalizes that she's gone through what she has in order to help her sisters through their troubles. She sings of the cycles that have trapped her—watching her father abuse her mother and finding herself suicidal and making the same mistakes. This song, too, has a distinctly hip hop fabric, built around a swirling groove sampling Queens vocalist Meli'sa Morgan, who had a string of Top Ten R&B hits when Blige was a teenager. By the end of the song, Blige's emphasis has changed—she tells her sisters, "I still have troubles too." This sort of eye-to-eye talk from the midst of trouble (not above it, not beyond it) was precisely what many fans seemed to miss on *Love & Life*.

While *Love & Life* talked of achieving perfection, the next two cuts, "Take Me as I Am" and "Baggage," embrace imperfection. On "Take Me as I Am," jazz pianist Lonnie Liston Smith's 1983 "A Garden of Peace" contributes both the piano fills and the melody, the singer telling of the abuse, gossip, and oppression she's faced and admitting she's gotten lost along the way. For "Baggage," Jimmy Jam and Terry Lewis offer a huge bass groove, lighter elements twinkling in the far distance, while Blige tries to explain why "one minute I'm so in love, and the next I can't stand you." As Blige's vocals cry and shout through the frustration, optimism fights its way forward with sunny backing vocals and dancing piano.

That optimism explodes into conviction with the full frontal assault of "Can't Hide from Luv." Keys and drums muscle forward, reminiscent of "Love" at the beginning of *No More Drama* but in this case built around Willie Hutch's cover of the Jackson 5's "I Wanna Be Where You Are." "It's coming to get ya!" Blige shouts, letting her lover know she's got to test his mettle, soaring through the song like a force of nature. Self-deprecation is turned into self-acceptance and a tribute to anyone willing to take her on.

"MJB da MVP" directs the lessons of the last three songs directly at the audience. In a remix of Compton rapper the Game's hit single with Detroit's 50 Cent, "Hate It or Love It" (itself built around Philly soul greats the Trammps' "Rubber Band"), Blige allies herself with the geographical centers of soul music as well as the class consciousness and candor of gangsta, made explicit by 50 Cent's rapped refrain, "The underdog's on top, and I'm gonna shine, homie, until my heart stops."

She then reaffirms her own story, touching on the places she's been with a list of song titles. She reaches for both "My Love" and "My Life," saying, "Whatcha gonna do without my life, my life, my life," admitting the importance of the song and album both to her fans and to her success. She finishes with thanks to everyone who has kept her going "to see me at a point in my life when I can actually call myself a queen." A testimony rooted in gospel, the humblest of brags becomes a rallying cry.

"Can't Get Enough" and "Ain't Really Love" walk relationship tightropes before the complete abandon of "I Found My Everything." On this cut, Blige pays bold tribute to Aretha Franklin. To do this, she calls on cowriter and producer Raphael Saadiq (lead singer of the decade-gone Oakland, California, trio Tony! Toni! Toné!) and Los Angeles's South Central Orchestra. When she sings, "Now my world feels so free," the chills she elicits explain why the connection to Franklin is inescapable. They are the soul of soul. Erasing the distinction between earthly and divine love, "I Found My Everything" places its emphasis right where it matters most—on the redemptive power of love itself.

A trilogy of string-laden conversations closes with "Father In You," a startlingly confessional admission that the singer has found a father figure in her new husband. It's quiet and reflective, as if being thought out as she finds the words—a steady forward rhythm with occasional pizzicato, wipers clearing the rain. "It was so hard trying to be a man and a woman," Blige sings, making it clear what she's really grateful for is a little relief.

The following quiet storm, "Alone," sets up the album's powerful conclusion by recapping what's come before, calling the lover out for fooling her—running her down, neglecting her, and changing on her. But this song quickly turns into both something old and something new. Sounding eerily like K-Ci Hailey on "Not Lookin'," singer Dave Young turns the table from the outset, declaring, "I gave you everything I had," and sighing, "Hmm. . . ." The two argue back and forth, coming to the same conclusion together—"I can't do this alone."

None of us can, and that is the theme of the U2 song that closes the album. Finally studio-recorded here, "One" works extraordinarily well as a conclusion because it takes the argumentative stance of the R&B that preceded it and focuses it outward, at a larger pop and rock audience. And, as Daphne Brooks pointed out, that's a tough conversation. It's there from the opening lines, Blige seizing on the realities that the dominant culture doesn't like to contemplate or doesn't know how to contemplate honestly. "Did I disappoint you? Or leave a bad taste in your mouth?" It only gains power when you hear her directly addressing Bono here, as she directly addressed Dave Young one song before, or K-Ci before.

Blige is doing what so many great black women artists have done since the early days of the blues: she's speaking truths that the outside world may not want to hear. The blow to her white audience may be softened by the fact that she says, "It's too late, tonight, to drag the past out into the light." But the power of the song is anything but diluted, and tomorrow is another day. On this gorgeous recording, when Blige sings "You ask me to enter," she makes it unforgettably plain she won't crawl. When she gets done preaching, the shared "carry each other" refrain sounds like the meaning of life.

The hidden track "Show Love" is perhaps "hidden" because it can't help but be anticlimactic after that finish. Still, it's hardly a throwaway. The intense rhythm track from the Neptunes-produced Jadakiss cut "Knock Yourself Out" pushes the notion of tough love as a weapon against armies of adversity. It's "My Life," "Keep Your Head," "Keep It Moving," and "Beautiful Day" rolled into a fight song. And her rat-a-tat vocal attack and the rubber-band bass do just what a fight song should—get you ready for whatever ring you're facing, even the ones that come with a wedding.

---

When I mentioned that I was writing a book about Mary J. Blige to singer-songwriter Narissa Bond, she told me I needed to talk to her brother, Jay Harris, whom she called "a superfan." (Quite a family, Harris's other sister, Cynthia Bond, released a debut novel, *Ruby*, that went on to be a 2015 Oprah's Book Club selection.) Harris worked as a youth counselor in Los Angeles. In the summer of 2014, he told me a story that brilliantly captured the size and scope of *The Breakthrough*:

> Two thousand seven seemed like the craziest and most spectacular year for Mary. Anytime I drove somewhere I would either hear another car blasting "Hate It or Love It [MJB da MVP]," "Enough Cryin," or "Be without You." Anytime I walked into a gas station or convenience store I would hear the hook of "Be without You" as someone's ringtone. Two thousand seven was a crazy and amazing year for me too. I had just recovered from months of chemotherapy and an exhausting and painful stem-cell transplant. Shortly after my victory, I spent my birthday in a psychiatric ward. I also spent the entire day waiting for Mary to perform at the Grammys. I managed to persuade all of the other patients in the unit to watch on the only television on the floor. Mary's emotional performance of "Be without You/Stay with Me" gave me hope for all of the possibilities of life. From seeing her first solo video for "You Remind Me" on BET in 1992 to watching her be recognized by the larger music world for her musical contributions on the Grammys, I knew that the hospital walls, and even feeling trapped in my own head, could not confine me.

# 20

# Growing Pains

*The Breakthrough* placed five singles on the charts, the last, "Take Me as I Am," coming out during Blige's summer 2006 *Breakthrough Experience* tour. That tour saw Blige using the new single's theme of self-acceptance as the key to her talk with the women in the audience. Blige performed as the musical guest on *Saturday Night Live* before her summer tour, and she came back to the show for a duet with Ludacris on his new single, "Runaway Love," released in November. In December, Blige released the greatest hits collection *Reflections (A Retrospective)*, which landed yet another single, "We Ride (I See the Future)" high in the R&B charts and introduced three other new tracks, including a duet with John Legend.

*The Breakthrough* snared over thirty major industry awards, and Blige received Grammys in 2007 for best R&B album and, for "Be without You" (the longest-charting R&B hit in four decades), best female R&B performance and best R&B song. In *Billboard* that following December, she told Gary Graff that the Grammy ceremony triggered her follow-up: "I started out with this concept of growing pains because that's how I was feeling during the [2007] Grammys: 'Am I good enough for this; do I really deserve all this in my life?' But something in my head said, 'Yes, you are. Now you're forced to rapidly grow up in this area [in] order to achieve and get the things you want.'"

Blige was certainly taking new strides with her career. Months before the Grammys, she'd traveled to South Africa for the opening of the Oprah Winfrey Leadership Academy for Girls, and she returned to Africa in October of 2007 for a few tour dates. She'd become very health conscious and started working out regularly (looking so much more fit she was rumored to have used steroids). She also set up a new label, Matriarch Records, with her husband and released a promo for an upcoming album featuring singer Dave Young (who'd sung on *The Breakthrough*).

And if all of these moves were about growing up, that didn't mean she left hip hop behind.

When Mary J. Blige was in the projects, hip hop threw a lifeline into her world by insisting there was a way to make life out of the broken pieces. However, even though that lifeline got her out of her specific trap, the world grew harder during Blige's post-"Drama" years—the country stayed perpetually at war, incarceration rates exploded, and the abandonment of all those homeowners after Katrina symbolized the rapidly expanding inequality. Even the GM plant where her demo had traded hands was long gone.

---

As if Blige is frantically mending what pieces she can, her 2007 album *Growing Pains* opens with hard hip hop—"Work That" and "Grown Woman" (with Ludacris) clear statements that being grown is owning the job in front of you. She ties marriage into the greater fight with "Roses," shouting "Welcome to the new definition of love!" over percussive sounds akin to shaking spray cans and racking guns. This is a record about what love means when the petals fall off the rose.

Blige used the Atlanta-based songwriting team Tricky Stewart and The-Dream, who had just had a monster hit with Rihanna's "Umbrella" (a single reportedly once destined for Blige), to anchor this album. From Blige's most determined-to-be-happy (and indeed effervescent) single, "Just Fine," to the naughty kink of the Usher duet, "Shake Down," to the "Roses" climax and the ambitious album closer, "Come to Me (Peace)," Blige, Stewart, and Dream scaffold the record's vision of art after marriage. The rest of the album fashions the pieces left over.

While Blige also calls on Bryan-Michael Cox of "Be without You," she gets most intimate working with Ne-Yo. "Fade Away" pulls together Ne-Yo and Norwegian production team Stargate for a big eighties soundscape with a cutting, guitar-driven pulse. The song is about wanting to disappear, ostensibly to hide the tears that plague a "perfect marriage," and the effect is scary, like looking into an abyss, well earning the string flourish that links it to the more hopeful meditation, "What Love Is."

Blige's definition of love is the most classically Ne-Yo of his collaborations here, silky and pop, with a seductive, friendly groove and the occasional chime. But the build on the refrain, a series of held notes on key, contradictory words—"It feels like *joy* and it feels like *pain*"—has the ring of an epic statement. "An excuse for dying, reason to live," love is the best and the worst; the only conclusion this string-adorned arrangement eventually finds is that we can't do without it. Love becomes a metaphor for life itself.

Appropriately enough, it's also a Ne-Yo-produced cut that Blige uses as the title track, "Work in Progress (Growing Pains)." This Wonder-esque reflection weaves plucks of string, beats, and backing vocals around a lifeline bass groove, tying sturdy, imperfect knots on rough seas stirred by raindrop computer bleeps, splashes of chimes, and sonic meteors. For a brief moment, Blige parts those seas to call, "Anybody knowing what it is to struggle . . . I'm with you, I feel you!" This becomes her jumping-off point for gospel testifying. "We're all the same," she cries, turning around that "we're not the same" from "One" to focus on the messy and real things we have in common. "Work in Progress" is a sonic collage the artist pieces together with the audience.

Built over the opening horns in the Emotions' "Key to My Heart," "Talk to Me" starts off lovingly confrontational, Blige stating she knows it's hard for a man "to reach out for help and to let down your guard." And she maintains the conversation with the

"If You Love Me?" sequel to "Be without You," featuring Brian-Michael Cox's circular groove, those "yes, yes, yes, yes" moments that punctuated that record, and "a few little things that I've been meaning to bring to your attention, partner." Being with you can still be a problem if either one of us quits putting energy into the relationship.

Blige always keeping the cliff's edge in sight, "Smoke" tells the story of a woman packing her lover's things because she wants him gone. She's hesitating because she's afraid of being alone, and she's also afraid to look in the mirror because she knows she shares the blame. This Ne-Yo-produced cut is a dark night of the soul, a piano in an echo chamber creating a big lonely room, keyboard suggesting the rain and bass and drums bringing thunder. Colored and shaded by sweeping strings, it's a theatrical piece coproduced by Syience (Reggie Perry, who went on to work with John Legend and Beyoncé, most notably with a similar grandeur on "If I Were a Boy"), and it exists on a slightly different plane than the rest of the record, surreal like a nightmare.

Blige closes with Tricky Stewart again and a bit of a sequel to "One." After all, "Come to Me (Peace)" is a tale of a couple's reconciliation that seems to want to grasp all the world's issues in its hands, to carry each other forward. Blige confronts the losses against pulsing bass, gaining drama from her restraint when she sings the first refrain's plea. The song takes on more color and size as she works the second verse and chorus in present tense, in the wreckage of a series of mistakes. Her vision of reconciliation in the last verse and refrain takes off through the repetition of the word "peace." And she closes no longer as the teacher but as the student, no longer the leader but a servant, her fading voice pleading, "Show me how to make peace with you."

Throughout this record, the answers have been found through hard work, and on "Roses," Blige sings, "This love stuff is demanding." That moment is strong, determined, and declamatory. But then she woefully admits, "Sometimes I need a hug." Angry as she is from the beginning to the end of this song, the very nucleus of this album, she's never seemed warmer—you can almost feel her heat, the touch of her breath. And, toward the end, when she finally starts shouting and laughing at her lover, when she's almost lost the last thread of control, it's precisely then, man or woman, you want to give her that hug. As round an artistic persona as has ever found its way on record, Mary J. Blige has always used her frailties as a way to draw listeners close. At this point, she's making it plain that owning one's own limits may be the only way to come together and take this thing higher.

A t 2:00 p.m. on January 18, 2009, two days before the inauguration of America's first black president, Barack Obama, two dozen headliners (including Beyoncé, Shakira, U2, Usher, Stevie Wonder, Bettye LaVette, and Mary J. Blige) performed for the televised concert *We Are One: The Obama Inaugural Celebration at the Lincoln Memorial*. Despite biting wind and temperatures well below freezing, over four hundred thousand people stood on the Mall before the memorial, many arriving six hours before.

Blige came on after Bruce Springsteen. Her backing band hidden in an orchestra pit, Blige stood alone on one of the memorial's plateaus, bundled against the cold in white gloves, a white scarf, and a plush white coat. On first look, she seemed small and vulnerable, but by the time she hit the chorus, her voice grew as big as her surroundings. She was gesturing and testifying by the second verse and began to travel down the steps with each "call on me, brother" break. The Mall rocking back and forth and clapping along with her, Blige pointed at and played off of the sea of individuals before her. From their side seats, the Obamas rocked back and forth, smiling like she was the reason they came.

"Call me, when you need a friend, when you need a friend," she cried at the end of the song, before concluding, "I'll be right there, be right there, be right there, be right there." And she raised her voice high and held that last note long, blessed assurance for America and for the new First Family.

The evening after the inauguration, a Mary J. Blige dressed in a sleek black evening gown hit the stage at the Obama Neighborhood

Inaugural Ball. The mood was every bit as giddy and excited as the previous performance had been reverential and comforting. Almost before the bubbling bass and keyboard riffs of "Just Fine" could be made out, Blige's voice boomed, "I don't know about yesterday, but today," she emphatically pointed at the floor, "I said today is just fine. Today is the beginning of no more separation, of no more segregation! See! It makes me wanna . . ." And she squealed before launching into the mile-a-minute lyric.

Strutting and pointing and waving at the VIPs filling the room, Blige shined bright, like the crystal feather earrings brushing the sides of her neck. As the performance went on, she grew more playful, fluffing her hair, swinging her rear, and kicking her heels high on the beat. Punching each note, she pushed herself harder and harder as the song went on, but the masterstroke came at the end. On her final statement, she shouted with all she had. "Fine!" The scream was not out of tune so much as free of it. She'd inhabited the song so fully that it became more than a song—a vehicle for cheering the birth of a new era.

# 21

# Stronger with Each Tear

It was an awkward and joyous moment when Mary J. Blige took center stage between Beyoncé and Mariah Carey. They stood alongside the top women in contemporary pop—Rihanna, Fergie, Carrie Underwood, Miley Cyrus, Nicole Scherzinger, Leona Lewis, Ashanti, Natasha Bedingfield, Ciara, and Keyshia Cole—for a live performance of the new L. A. Reid and Babyface collaboration "Just Stand Up!" to benefit the American Association for Cancer Research. The September 5, 2008, live performance was shown on all three major TV networks, part of a campaign that raised over $100 million for cancer research, the first of a series of biannual telethons to fight cancer on a variety of research fronts at once.

The thirteen women who crowded together, all wearing black "Stand Up to Cancer" T-shirts, couldn't really move much—just sway to the beat and keep rhythm with their palms—but the artlessness of the staging felt appropriate. Importantly, from Beyoncé's opening to the playful back-and-forth between Cyrus and Rihanna to Blige's climactic trade-off with Carey, the music was heartfelt and moving. "You don't gotta be a prisoner in your mind," Blige boomed, pointing at the crowd and bolstering the ad hoc group with her personal testimonial. Beyoncé beamed at the woman next to her, relieved to see the team's ball go out of the park. Though Blige's most recent album had only sold about a third as many copies as *The Breakthrough*, she was still as much of-the-moment as anyone on that stage. She was likely the busiest.

She'd just finished her European tour to support *Growing Pains*, and she had a new single coming out, guesting with Musiq Soulchild. She was also working on her role as a bartender in the upcoming Tyler Perry movie *I Can Do Bad All by Myself*. In that role, she would act alongside up-and-comer Taraji P. Henson and a musical hero, Gladys Knight. Knight and Blige would turn in the two climactic musical performances in the film—Knight's own "The Need to Be" and Blige's new title song for the movie, a gorgeous piano-based and string-laden collaboration with Ne-Yo.

Blige's music was featured in new singles for two other films in 2009, "Stronger," for the LeBron James documentary *More than a Game*, and "Color," for director Lee Daniels's dramatic portrait of a troubled high school girl, *Precious*, a film that would go on to win five Independent Spirit Awards and six Academy Award nominations, including best film, best director, best actress, and best supporting actress. *Precious* was based on the book *Push*, the first novel by Sapphire, which established an important link between Blige's work and a burgeoning literary movement spearheaded by black women authors, a movement that, in terms of Blige's work, was becoming all the more important as black women's voices grew increasingly scarce in popular music.

All three of these movies came out in the run-up to Blige's ninth studio album (as did a Christmas single with Andrea Bocelli), but 2009's *Stronger with Each Tear* was the first Mary J. Blige album to inspire generally lukewarm domestic response. The record sold well the first week (like the previous two, released just before Christmas), and it received gold certification by spring, but only its album-release single, "I Am," cracked the US R&B Top Ten. This drop-off signaled the first clear sign that pop radio might no longer be much interested in the thirty-eight-year-old star.

At the same time, a combination of factors could explain the new lack of enthusiasm among critics. Some of the music seemed like a retread of things Blige had done before—"The One" was thematically almost identical to "I Am." And "Good Love" was a bit of a generic dance floor come-on, give or take the Ne-Yo-penned catchiness and a rap by T.I.

---

Still, Blige's shortest album, *Stronger with Each Tear*, has considerable merit for its concise punches. The album starts with a blast of percussive air courtesy of Florida production team the Runners before building a dark and pulsing atmosphere of expectation. On "Tonight," Akon's presence as a writer and producer helps Blige build the song's epic quality, her wordless backing vocals reaching for Africa. The shuddering soundtrack sounds like a small boat crossing dark waters to get there.

"Give me a little more of myself," Blige says to engineer Pat Thrall at the opening of "Said and Done." The first song on the record to deal with everyday messiness may be both confession and positive self-talk, but its harpsichord-springy bounce offers another reason to dance. Written and produced with singer and rapper Ryan Leslie, this song is less hot and heavy and more fun than what's come before. A propulsive dance song built around a groove that's perpetually restarting, "Good Love" keeps the forward movement exciting. T.I. all but steals the show with his spirited rap—the smile you can hear on him radiates throughout the production.

After T.I. beckons a woman into the night, "I Feel Good" dramatizes what happens next. On this Ne-Yo collaboration, Blige is a princess (or a queen) stepping out of the darkness into the light, her dress cutting through a line of people who resent her, and she shakes it off because she knows she has a right to this moment. "I feel good," she sings, "like the moon is shining just for me." With starlight keys and strings over ripples of piano, the arrangement makes you believe it.

Blige again calls on most of the "Be without You" team for "I Am," an extension of the self-assurance that comes before addressing the trade-off that is marriage. Blige tells her partner,

"If you feel the need to leave, just know"—and she hangs onto that open vowel long enough to fully get his attention—and then she sings a litany of things that amount to "ain't nobody gonna love you better, boy, than I am." If it wasn't clear before, she's underscoring the point—this is a record about the self-worth necessary to fulfill a commitment.

"Each Tear" drives this point home. A rootedness in pulsing bass ties the theatrical scope of the cut's orchestration to "Tonight"'s world music vibe. The audience now is clearly the sisters, who, like Blige, make mistakes and learn from that process. Strings paint a starry sky, each of the song's tears falling against glimmering waves of piano and propelling toward a promise of dawn. This "what doesn't kill you makes you stronger" mantra generates both delicacy and epic sweep.

"We Got Hood Love" accepts the hard truths that have led up to this moment. Yes, this couple fights worse than they should—"I be cussing, I be screaming"—but no one touches them like they touch each other. Acoustic guitar opens the song, giving it the timeless feel of a madrigal, and accompanied by Trey Songz's high, sweet vocal echoing Blige's thoughts, this song celebrates a rough-and-tumble sweetness. If this is self-help talk, it's of the class-conscious variety.

The following song about keeping house is every bit as fun as it is serious. "Let the piano man play," Blige calls out, and an ornery feel-good vibe springs forth. Starting as a late-night call to an "other woman," "Kitchen" works the metaphor of a woman's territory with playful references to limited cabinet space, the fridge as a step toward the stove, and a boiling point as the call to direct action. Cowritten by The-Dream and coproduced by Tricky Stewart, this record uses contemporary keyboard sounds—bass blurts, chimes, and beats—to update a classic R&B arrangement. The result is a delight of a set piece that gets real pragmatic about marriage—"I consider him an investment/Trynna take my man is like trynna take my money." It's a domestic sequel to the Miracles' "Shop Around."

In a similarly classic vein, "In the Morning" suggests "Will You

Still Love Me Tomorrow" as a grown woman's question after another hard-fought night. Cowritten by another sister team, Anesha and Antea Birchett, and coproduced by Ron Fair, this record brings big horns, strings, and piano to bear on a rhythmically fast-shifting and hard-yielding vocal. When Blige finally tells the man to "just . . . love me in the morning," anyone in a long-term relationship has to grasp the existential fear.

On an album about self-care as a sort of quest, the tour de force is also the most distinctively individual statement, another Raphael Saadiq collaboration, "Color." Bluesy guitar, warm fire, and some almost whispered backing vocals insist on restraint, while Blige's voice works every possibility trying to explain a life-changing shift in vision. It's seeing colors for "the very first time," but though some of the colors are as specific as a "baby-blue" sky, they also take intangible forms, like "the first sign of spring." She sees rosebuds and promises to hold them "forever and ever and ever and ever and ever." Though Blige's voice splashes color throughout the mix, she leaves the portrait nuanced, pulling back when in the past she might have taken off and run. The result is every bit as delicate as it is moving. A record that started with restraint ends with restraint, the sweet potential all the more powerful for being savored.

This portrait of a young Mary J. Blige captures the girl who launched her career by covering Anita Baker in a shopping mall recording booth. She wasn't yet eighteen when she first signed to Uptown Records, and she spent the four years leading up to her debut honing her chops as a backing vocalist for Jeff Redd, Father MC, Grand Puba, and Christopher Williams. Courtesy of Lisa Leone.

Blige at the Schlobohm Housing Projects in 2010. Blige lived in these tough Yonkers high-rises from the age of nine until her first record started making money over a decade later. In this *Oprah* segment documenting her return, she stated, "I could have been dead, you know, because of this environment, but because of this environment, I'm alive, too." Photo courtesy *OWN*.

Sean Combs, Blige, and sister LaTonya working on the career-defining album *My Life*. They were all in their early twenties and could not have imagined the level of success that lay just ahead. Photo: Chucky Thompson.

With the debut video for *My Life*, Blige shed her tomboy image and embraced a chic-but-street look dubbed "ghetto fabulous." Over the next two decades, she gave further nuance to the concept, her style announcing both roots and trajectory. Video directed by Sean Combs and Harold "Hype" Williams.

Blige declaring "No More Drama" at the 44th Annual Grammy Awards in 2002. Her gospel-powered, stage-front intensity challenged the staid conventions of the industry ceremony. Photo: AP.

Blige all but stealing the show at VH1 Diva Duets in the spring of 2003. With a new marriage and a new outlook, her shows from this area would define (and document, with two concert DVDs) her greatness as a live performer. Photo: AP.

Whitney Houston and Blige at Arista Records President Clive Davis's after-party for *VH1 Divas Live* in April 1999. As a crossover success comparable only to Aretha Franklin, Houston lay important groundwork for Blige and became a staunch supporter of the young artist. Blige would credit Houston's death in 2012 with her own renewed fight for sobriety. Photo: Shutterstock.

*That song "Runaway Love" she did with Ludacris,*
*I remember it made me cry, and still makes me cry, actually.*
*It always seems to me that she tries to speak to people*
*who are lost, especially women. And although she only*
*sings the chorus in that song, it's like it has the power that*
*Mary J. Blige brings to her own songs.*

**Itzel Lopez, student, artist, dreamer from Guadalajara, Mexico**
**(2014 interview with the author)**

# 22

# Hard Times Come Again No More

Even as Blige's pop-charting career began to take its first hard hits, her stature seemed to grow in new ways. She'd started the decade playing a convict's mother in the 2001 film *Prison Song*, and she'd appeared off Broadway as a former death row inmate in the play *The Exonerated*. She'd since played a number of roles on various television series, including herself on *Entourage* and *30 Rock*, and now she had a key role in Tyler Perry's new movie. Aside from becoming an increasingly formidable actress, Blige was becoming a mainstream American icon. In January of 2010, she delivered a performance that embraced the artistic challenge that comes with that status.

The telethon had come together quickly in the ten days after Haiti's January 10, 2010, earthquake, a disaster that affected more than 3.5 million people, injured more than 300,000, and killed at least 220,000. Gathered by George Clooney, A-list Hollywood celebrities—everyone from Tom Hanks to Halle Berry to Clint Eastwood and Denzel Washington—agreed to appear on the *Hope for Haiti Now* telecast alongside Stevie Wonder, Beyoncé, Shakira, Justin Timberlake, and Madonna, musicians enlisted by organizers Wyclef Jean and Joel Gallen, the director of the broadcast.

The original plan called for Mary J. Blige to reprise her performance of "One" with U2, a highlight of the 2005 Katrina fundraiser *Shelter from the Storm*. When that plan fell through, Gallen suggested Blige sing the Stephen Foster song "Hard Times Come Again No More."

On one level, it was an audacious suggestion, the Queen of Hip Hop Soul singing a parlor song by the preeminent songwriter for blackface minstrelsy. On the other hand, minstrelsy does lay much of the groundwork for American popular culture, and "Hard Times" has managed to escape the cultural baggage of "Beautiful Dreamer" or "Old Folks at Home (Swanee River)."

During the telethon performance, Blige appeared on a darkened stage wearing a simple black dress, a bold silhouette defined by strong shoulders. Her blonde hair was cut short but swooped upward in an elegant wave. Her regal, caramel-colored features worked to smooth the furrow of her brow, her eyes closing as if in prayer.

She may have been counting measures, but she seemed to wordlessly ruminate over the melody against snapping fingers and an unhurried piano intro. With the first line, "Let us pause in life's pleasures and count its many tears," she established the act of singing a 156-year-old song to eighty-three million viewers as something natural and intimate.

At this point in the show, the tone of *Hope for Haiti Now* had been appropriately somber—Bruce Springsteen singing a whispery "We Shall Overcome," Stevie Wonder offering compassion with "Bridge Over Troubled Water," John Legend fingering the jagged grain of "Motherless Child"—but Blige's "Hard Times" gathered strength from the pain. As she began to use her hands to dismiss those hard times and point at the "frail forms fainting at the door," a smile played in her features. A gospel flutter took her hand, and that hand soon turned to a clenched fist as she repeated, "hard times," testifying to the burden while rallying for the fight.

As is so often the case, the song's bridge was key. When the Roots' "Captain" Kirk Douglas began a probing blues guitar lead, Blige moaned the blues along with him, the prelude to a musical charge. She used her voice like a horn searching for a solo—casting about in different directions, whooping and yeahing and then shouting. The guitar was soon overrun by the power of her vocal. She went into the last verse and chorus with an air of renewal.

The dynamic of the vocal had now become a sustained shout, reaching higher and deeper and hitting harder. On the next refrain, she bit down on the "g" in "again," and then she invoked Mavis Staples's growl, paying homage to both the arrangement she borrowed and one of the most important voices in American music, indeed a voice synonymous with the soul era and civil rights. When she growled on the next refrain, her voice had jumped higher, and it danced all over the beat.

With that old parlor song, she traced a bold line connecting her vision as a black woman from both the projects and the sticks to this music from America's first popular songwriter, Stephen Foster, a white man working in a racist tradition. Foster, in his way and time and admittedly with thick blinders (Foster never even visited the South he so often romanticized), and Blige, singing his "Hard Times Come Again No More," were talking about what's left out of the American story. In an America founded on a dream, a self-proclaimed model of freedom and equal opportunity for all, Foster was writing about the people who were struggling merely to survive. Having spent a career fighting the forces that threaten to kill the human spirit, Mary J. Blige tied the struggles of everyday Haitians to her own struggles and to those of all who are left out of the American dream.

With each breath of that telethon performance, Blige used Foster to invite Americans of all races to attend to what we want to deny. When those prayerful eyes opened, she called us to "all sup sorrow with the poor," hanging onto that "all" so that we knew everyone listening was indeed the intended audience. When Blige reached the first refrain, "There's a song that will linger/Forever in our ears/Of hard times/Come again no more," it was clear that she found in Foster's lines an overarching statement of her own purpose.

# 23

# My Life II ... The Journey Continues (Act 1)

Since Hurricane Katrina, 2009 had been the only year Mary J. Blige failed to play the Fourth of July weekend Essence Music Festival in New Orleans. She returned to that stage in 2010, and she toured in both the U.K. and the United States through the fall. She also performed in a number of award ceremonies that year, another fund-raiser for Haiti, and an appearance on Letterman to perform "I Am," following up a 2009 performance of "Stronger."

Blige's movie work continued to keep her busy. Blige was inspired by the ambivalence of the three black women central to *The Help*. Because of those characters, she cowrote a song, "The Living Proof," for the soundtrack. She also shot her performance for the upcoming film of the Broadway play *Rock of Ages*. It was a good time for her. In January 2012, she told the *Windy City Times*'s Chris Azzopardi, "It was a lot of fun going to work . . . because my role as Justice is to be a strip club owner. She's a lot of fun but she's strong, and we sang some of the really good classic songs from the '80s like 'Any Way You Want It' and 'Here I Go Again.' It was just fun, man. The little part I did with Tom Cruise? Amazing!" Amazing or not, Blige's voice certainly made both of those songs more fun than they would have been otherwise.

But Blige was mostly busy recording in the two years before 2011's *My Life II . . . The Journey Continues (Act 1)*. She cut fifty songs for the seventeen-song release, which was why the album release received the "Act 1" subtitle. As if feeling the full range of her strengths, Blige transitioned to the third decade of her career with music as exciting and challenging as anything she'd done before. In some ways, it was both her most hook-laden and her most sophisticated record. It also lived up to the title's promise, approaching her story as a journey of self-discovery and gaining the ground necessary to point a way forward.

The fact that it was impatiently reviewed by critics said more about the growing limits of contemporary popular music criticism than it did about the music. The fact that it didn't chart as high as any of her records after *My Life* said less about Blige than the hazards of increasingly fragmented radio, particularly when the Top Forty becomes almost exclusively preteen territory—a home for viral video acts, former Disney child stars, and winners of TV talent shows.

The contrast between the conditions surrounding the original *My Life* and its sequel are vivid. In 1994, thirty-seven of the year's Top One Hundred records featured women, and twenty-four of those songs featured black women artists. Seventeen years later, the Year-End Top One Hundred included only two black women, Rihanna and Nicki Minaj, with their own singles, and Janelle Monáe singing on a record by the white alternative rock band Fun. Exactly ten years younger than Blige, Beyoncé had one Top Twenty single, "Best Thing I Never Had," but that didn't make the year-end totals. Beyoncé did not have another Top Ten single until "Drunk In Love" in 2013. Pop radio was no longer a place where a Queen of Hip Hop Soul could be expected to thrive.

In 2012, Gotye and Adele had stand-out singles with both a pop and an adult contemporary appeal, and Carly Rae Jepsen and One Direction could serve the bubblegum crowd. Flo Rida and Maroon 5 could be expected to stoke a party, while Rihanna, Katy Perry, Nicki Minaj, and Ellie Goulding would complicate that party in interesting ways.

Blige's record wasn't invited, but it would have added some weight to the conversation. With five of the hardest-hitting tracks she'd ever recorded up front, Blige's late 2011 record matched the energy level of anything on the pop charts over the year that followed, while insisting that music not only is about life's deepest struggles but it also has the capacity to build upon twenty years of perspective on those struggles.

---

She takes her listeners back to the beginning on her first "Intro" cut since *Love & Life*, Blige sharing another phone call with Combs. This time, however, she's made the call. When Combs tries to tell her to keep in mind "that *My Life I* is a classic, so if you're going to do it, you better come with it, girl," she immediately replies, "It's not a competitor, it's a sequel and an extension of how far we've come."

Several things are worth noting here. Blige is in control of this conversation. She's being gracious enough to consult Combs about this project because it's the right thing to do. And her focus is not on competition, with Combs or with herself. As with all of the work in her second decade, this is a record about, as she puts it here, "how to navigate." Thematically, that doesn't give it the romantic flash of her younger work, but it gives her increasingly nuanced substance.

The album's journey starts with "Feel Inside," a daring leap into darkness. "I want to make you happy," Blige's voice rings out, a party cry with all the pain of a blues shout. Over a sort of spondaic rhythm, two stresses launching and relaunching the song, Nas tells the story of a relationship that's given up on itself. Blige comes back in with verses constantly building in intensity, the only relief a sweetly sung chorus with bone-tired reflections like, "I'm to the point where I don't know what I believe in." The only hope in this song comes with the effort to communicate, the insistent rhythm, the enchanting colors in the refrain.

To ramp the record over this impasse, Blige brings in her rapping ego, Brook Lynn, for "Midnight Drive." Brook expresses the impulsiveness, the immediacy, and, yes, the dangers of eroticism in a way Ms. Blige can't quite do with her own persona. (Though this song is ostensibly about a wife getting home to her husband, it has all the thrill of something more clandestine.) It's Blige's first rock-and-roll highway song, and it fits because it's every bit as slinky as whatever sports car she might fantasize about driving— whether Prince's Little Red Corvette or Pebbles's Mercedes.

Replacing the fast car imagery with a rocket ship, "Next Level" uses a bouncy ascending keyboard line to suggest perpetual take-off. What's most notable about this song, however, is that it takes such fantastic imagery and applies it to a married couple staying home and exploring what they're more inclined to take for granted. And the significance of that theme should not be rushed past—committed love as an infinity of potential within limits. Playfulness being key, this duet works, in no small part, because Busta Rhymes's clown prince image allows him to do things like rhyme "cuddle" with "space shuttle."

Like the dance floor's just come off the ground, the cover of Chaka Khan's "Ain't Nobody" takes almost the same synth-heavy arrangement and elevates it, Blige singing, "And now we're flying through the stars." Her voice sounds stronger than ever, blasting like a house singer. Hanging onto the last note to emphasize the "sure" of a committed love, "We cannot measure!"

Although it was released as the first single, "25/8" makes more sense at this point on the album than it does in isolation on the radio. On the radio, it was a bouncy, hook-laden "Eight Days a Week"–themed single. On the album, it's a climax topping off five hard-driving commitments to love after marriage. As she pledges her love from "the north to the south pole . . . every area code all over the globe," Blige's vocal punches come so hard and fast that the occasional dynamic shifts—stops and starts, what sounds like a whole orchestra bouncing off the walls dropping down to a single flute or bass line—call to mind James Brown being halfway walked off stage in his cape. Then she drops the cape again, runs back to the mic, and cries one more time, "Twenty-four hours ain't enough!" Interestingly, this song claims an all but imperceptible sample of the O'Jays' "Now That We Found Love," underscoring the central theme of the record, and much of the second half of Blige's career—"What are we gonna do with it?"

Next, "Don't Mind," the record's first slowdown, focuses on the fragile state of simply holding onto it. With an ambiguous bass line and a nervous skitter of keyboard, a valentine becomes a reflection on love and risk. The last line sums up the danger—"Saying I love you is giving you strength to break my heart, but I'm trusting you."

So far, everything has sounded of a piece—Blige holding hard to the musical reins. "No Condition" is something else. It starts cinematically, a tide of strings lapping up against piano. Then Kevin Cossom's backing vocal kicks in, like one of Akon's wordless calls. That reference seems very intentional, lending grandeur to this end-of-a-relationship ballad.

"In another life or space," Blige sings, giving up on this one. She sounds like she's crossing back across those waters from "Tonight," reflecting on her reasons for leaving. It's a stunning performance because, in defeat, this character shows she knows how to make her exit and go on with her own life.

Blige's collaboration with Drake, who raps the title role on "Mr. Wrong," was the most popular single on the album, hitting number ten on the US R&B charts. And that makes sense, not only because that was a big year for Drake but also because it is archetypal Blige. It's that real-world thing that allows her to falter, even as her loved ones say, "Don't do it, Mary." Either way, it's the inescapable relationship blues, encapsulated in the hook, "Bad boys ain't no good/ Good boys ain't no fun."

And, of course, part of the appeal of "Mr. Wrong" is the fun implied by that lyric. He breaks her heart, but "we got a special thing going on." Not only is the mid-tempo pace begging singers to join in, but the song's stuttering electronic breaks, stops and starts, keep it seductive. It's zero coincidence that Jim Jonsin is one of the producers here. Three years prior, Jonsin's Lil Wayne hit "Lollipop" worked much the same minimalist hypnosis about another Mr. Wrong.

If "No Condition" and "Mr. Wrong" stand as polar outcomes

to relationship troubles, "Why" sounds like the more ambivalent ground most couples walk—"We both said that things will change, but it's still the same shade of gray." Rick Ross is used to interesting effect here. His raspy brags are answered by Blige's questions, "Why, why, why, can't we get it right?"

The notion of a man and woman living in different worlds gets explored directly in the duet with Beyoncé, "Love a Woman." It's worth stopping a second and considering the significance of this collaboration. The Recording Industry Association of America's Artist of the Decade, and the top-selling singles artist of the decade, in other words, the Queen of Pop, Beyoncé, is collaborating with the Queen of Hip Hop Soul. And even though they are both R&B artists rooted in hip hop, it's hard to imagine two queens with more distinctively different images. In 2009, Sasha Frere-Jones called Beyoncé "pop's A student," pointing out how "she never drifts to the back of the classroom." Mary J. Blige is not only the girl from the back of the classroom; she's the one who dropped out.

The ways in which the two mesh here, then, are noteworthy. Their voices find common ground with a trumpet-like melisma somewhere between a blues moan and a torch singer's seduction. And they both agree on a long list of needs, best captured by one of Blige's opening lines—"A woman needs so much more than what a man can say." Finally, they both find common ground turning the song's climax into a statement of sexual power that stops just shy of being too naughty for prime time—"Kiss her real slow, and get down and blow her mind."

The three songs that close the album offer a kind of genre-free popular song that forecasts the many frontiers Blige has ahead of her. At the same time, they plumb the depths of a quest that has ended with dubious outcomes. The fact that Blige finds hope in this reflection suggests the road ahead may well be the most interesting part of the story yet.

The progression starts at its darkest point. "Empty Prayers" offers tortured thoughts over the sort of deliberate piano playing that almost suggests the song is being written as she sings it, as she sorts through her feelings about someone who has chosen to quit listening. Guitar travels keyboard intergalactics, but quietly, like a falling star in an old Hank Williams song. The effect is as whispery as those prayers she's singing about. The one crescendo in the song apologizes for wasting time on a man who doesn't have the "decency to intervene" on her behalf.

As the next step in the same story, "Need Someone" finds the woman accepting that the lovers may not be able to provide for each other's needs. Featuring acoustic guitar, little more than brushes of snare, and those piano and strings, this troubled love letter is palpably warm.

The generosity of that moment allows the album to end with a new beginning. "The Living Proof," written with Hollywood composer Thomas Newman and composing team The Underdogs, yet again sums up the Mary J. Blige story, but it looks forward. The church piano that backs her vocals speaks to her own Georgia roots, as do the essentially gospel ambitions of the song.

The song begins with the singer bracing herself for "a long, long journey" ahead, reminding herself and her listeners to be thankful "the worst is over." How can she say that after announcing the future will be filled with struggle? Because her stories and the stories of others give her "the living proof" that she can persevere.

When she explains the job ahead of her, her voice rises on the phrase "my people," those she shares her troubles with and those who give her strength. On the song's climactic build, she shouts with the ecstasy of one discovering a truth revealed, "I know where I'm goin'/'Cause I know where I've been." In this moment, she sums up the value of history, both personal and political—from our civil rights to our individual dreams.

---

A few days after the album came out, Blige chose "Need Someone" to sing at the Fayetteville, North Carolina, Crown Coliseum for World Wrestling Entertainment's annual *Tribute to the Troops*. Despite all the stars and stripes glitz of the occasion, Blige's performance was intimate. She wore a simple white suit, her hair down. It was all about her voice over acoustic guitars, some strings for support.

The cutaways to soldiers and their families from Fort Bragg made a clear statement about the needs we hide behind our masks. Couples clutched one another to lines like, "You need someone to hold you and tell you everything is all right." That live moment touched so deeply it hurt . . . Potentially, it started a little healing.

# 24

# A Mary Christmas

On November 2, 2012, Blige performed for yet another disaster relief telethon, and it was one that hit particularly close to home. In late October of that year, Hurricane Sandy marched up the Eastern Seaboard and devastated the New York/New Jersey area she had lived in almost all of her life. When she sang "The Living Proof" for *Hurricane Sandy: Coming Together*—on stage alone, dressed in a simple blue suit, her hair pulled back—the moment was particularly moving. In his review of the event, the *New York Times*'s Jon Pareles wrote, "When Ms. Blige sang 'The Living Proof,' she changed 'I' to 'we,' transforming a song about individual survival into one of shared perseverance and performing it with gospel-rooted drama." The gospel was particularly evident when she threw out her arm to repeat the line, "They just don't make it through," before reassuring, "But look at us, look at us, we're the living proof."

After the song, the camera pulled back to show emcees Brian Williams and Jon Stewart looking deferential and moved. Blige hugged them both, long and real. The whole performance had, simultaneously, felt like words of encouragement and self-talk. Of course, that intense connection between the personal and the political (in the absolute broadest sense of the word) is nothing new for Blige; it's the way she operates. The significance of Pareles's observation is really to point out how Blige made it clear to the largest audience possible that this song is about her hopes for them.

Blige had her own rough year before the hurricane. It started the night before the Grammys, on February 11, with the shocking death of Blige's stalwart friend for over a decade, Whitney Houston. Houston had drowned in her bathtub as the result of a heart attack brought on by cocaine use. On the February 29 episode of *The View*, Blige talked frankly about her relationship with Houston. "I got a chance to express with her what I felt about her, and how important she is, and how I don't like to see her like that, and she's better than that." But Blige understood Houston too. At one point, she said, "You never know you're addicted until you're up late nights running out on the street as Mary J. Blige looking for it."

Blige credited Houston's funeral with making her stop drinking. In 2013, she told the *Guardian*'s Caroline Sullivan, "Being that close to someone you loved so dearly, in a coffin—it freaked me out. It made me realize the importance of my own life. I didn't stop overnight—it was a process, and then it was a dead stop."

Her new level of sobriety arrived in the face of more challenges. Her spring and summer were spent trying to straighten out the financial troubles of her girls' support organization, Foundation for the Advancement of Women Now (FFAWN), which had failed to provide promised scholarships and even to pay ancillary musicians who had worked a large benefit for the organization. In May 2012, she told *E! News*, "As founder and CEO of FFAWN, I am ultimately responsible for anything that goes wrong. The problem is that I didn't have the right people in the right places doing the right things. . . . This should have never been allowed to happen, but it did and now we are fixing it," adding, "FFAWN is not closing down. . . . Their goal is to get the foundation back on track, rectify outstanding issues, and make good on all of FFAWN's obligations."

This financial trouble interfered with her ability to promote *My Life II*, which was turning out to be anything but the blockbuster it set out to be. In fact, it was her lowest-selling album to date. When she did launch *The Liberation Tour*, with coheadliner D'Angelo, they only played eighteen dates. She would pick up a few more the following year.

The year 2013 started on a more hopeful note. In February, Blige played Betty Shabazz, the wife of Malcolm X, in the Lifetime movie *Betty and Coretta*. Aside from the obvious significance of that lead role, Blige acted opposite Angela Bassett, who, twenty years before, had played Shabazz in the Spike Lee movie *Malcolm X*. Though the movie was minimally reviewed, Blige's plainspoken performance was powerful, investing the film's core character with understated humility and warmth.

That film landed her an eleventh *Vibe* cover, but that was a brief bright spot in a tough season. It was a spring of showdowns between the IRS and hip hop. Three children of now-deceased Sylvia Robinson, founder of Sugar Hill Records, were sentenced to probation for back taxes, and Lauryn Hill was sentenced to prison for failing to pay federal income taxes. Blige was hit with a $3.4 million lien by the federal government and then over $900,000 were assessed due to the state of New Jersey. Blige responded as she did to the FFAWN troubles, proactively, in this case working, a lot, to raise money. While Mary J. Blige had always been extraordinarily active—making her own music, playing tours and benefits, and recording backing vocals and remixes for other artists—little compared to the whirlwind that came next.

Between the summer of 2013 and the summer of 2014, Mary J. Blige finished the last leg of her *My Life II* tour. She also sang "The Star-Spangled Banner" at Fenway Park for the World Series (and again at the Thanksgiving Day game between the Dallas Cowboys and the Oakland Raiders). She performed in the 2013 Nobel Peace Prize Concert. She released a Christmas album and then recorded and broadcast a Christmas special for HSN, did a round of other Christmas specials, including Michael Bublé's and the *CMA Country Christmas*, and even played an angel in the film version of the Langston Hughes play *Black Nativity*. She also recorded duets with the British dance act Disclosure and with singer Sam Smith. Then she topped things off by recording and releasing the soundtrack album for the film *Think Like a Man Too* just before headlining the Essence Music Festival in New Orleans. By June 2014, she'd paid off those New Jersey taxes, but she wasn't letting up, in July talking about an upcoming release to be recorded in the UK called *The London Sessions*.

The press's superficial coverage of the Christmas album and the soundtrack (neither of which was widely reviewed) suggested an assumption that this work was desperate or, worse, uninspired. After *Think Like a Man Too*, the *Los Angeles Times* ran with a headline, "Mary J. Blige has a new album out. Has anyone noticed?" attached to an article giving the record lukewarm praise and speculating, "This might be her laziest album ever." Still, the album charted at number thirty in the *Billboard* Top Two Hundred and hit number six on the hip hop/R&B chart because Blige has a core audience that trusts her enough to listen to the music, not the reviewers. Fortunately, Blige knows this audience is out there, and she works hard to maintain their respect.

---

Blige took a risky approach to the Christmas record: she played it quiet. As she told interviewers before it came out, she had no interest in reinventing the Christmas standards she was singing. And she didn't. As she always had with her covers, Blige paid tribute to the originals, in this case generally Christmas carols and pop standards that predate both the hip hop and the soul eras. The one soul standard here, Donny Hathaway's "This Christmas," seemed subdued next to the original. Conversely, the song most contemporary to Blige's career, "Mary, Did You Know?" (released as a country single by Kathy Mattea in 1993 and to even more success by Kenny Rogers and Wynonna Judd in 1996), stood out most on first listen, in part because it began as the quietest record here, essentially Blige's voice over piano, and that core held when the strings kicked in and her voice shot the moon in a way it hadn't elsewhere.

Upon the first few plays, the subtlety of the album made it hard to fully appreciate. Celine Dion producer David Foster further contributed to the opacity of this record by avoiding contemporary hooks in the arrangements—everything sounds a little (or a lot) like the orchestration for a seventies TV variety show. That said, the resulting album spoke volumes about Blige as an artist and raised some essential questions about musical boundaries.

Of Blige, Foster stated in the liner notes, "She's reliving her childhood with this album," and Blige echoed this sentiment in many interviews, particularly singling out Nat King Cole's "The Christmas Song" as the music that "signaled Christmastime was coming." In those same liner notes she listed *How the Grinch Stole Christmas* and three Rankin/Bass animated specials, starting with *The Year without a Santa Claus*, as her favorite shows to watch as a kid. None of this was surprising, of course, but it underscored the fact that Blige grew up in the heart of the same American pop culture as most kids her age. That Christmas culture was very much forged in a sensibility that, at least once a year, blurred cultural lines. Even today, the Christmas season throws everything before and after the rock-and-roll and hip hop revolutions into one big mix.

---

L istening to *A Mary Christmas* makes it very clear that Blige wanted to make an extension of that Nat King Cole record she loved so much as a kid. Every cut here is refined and understated, meant to be soothing to any listener, particularly those beat-up and broke-down and hoping for some sense of the peace promised by the season. Sure, Blige throws in a blue note here and there, and a hint of a gospel push once or twice, but the fact that she maintains such restraint from beginning to end is an artistic goal (and a remarkable one) achieved. Interestingly enough, Blige's restraint seems to have reined in Foster's bombastic tendencies as a producer. Nothing here feels over the top. Of course, since most listeners don't turn to Blige searching for restraint, it's also worth noting that she doesn't lack for intensity either.

Part of the purpose of this record, after all, is to throw the biggest

Christmas party she can, and to do so, there's a little spectacle to the proceedings. She puts the rhythm number "Little Drummer Boy" up front, although instead of bouncing on some funky bass line, she maintains the bright, flickering light of her voice as a relatively small beacon in an arrangement dominated by choir and orchestral strings. On "Rudolph, the Red-Nosed Reindeer," she manages a turn as a big band singer, scatting against the horn section and making it all sound surprisingly effortless. She even manages a moving "Petit Papa Noël" in French. Then there's her duet with Barbra Streisand on "When You Wish Upon A Star," which both women handle with great delicacy and warmth, and though Barbra reaches for the rafters a couple of times, Mary's grounding gives such moments even more drama.

All of the duets here work well, as did those from the Christmas specials. In fact, watching Blige sing with Michael Bublé or Sugarland's Jennifer Nettles in those specials only underscored what an empathetic duet partner Blige has become over years collaborating with so many of her peers. Here, she engages in interlocking vocals with British pop star Jessie J on "Do You Hear What I Hear?" and joins Marc Anthony with the bilingual "Noche de Paz (Silent Night)." The fireworks finale, though still restrained, is her many-textured call and response with the Clark Sisters on "The First Noel."

But the moments that most define this album are among the most traditional, her childhood favorite, "Have Yourself a Merry Little Christmas" followed by Rodgers and Hammerstein's "My Favorite Things." Blige goes for the smoothness of Nat King Cole with "Have Yourself," but her voice still sands some fresh emotion from the song. Particularly poignant is the way she halts after the line "Through the years we all will be together," lightly laughing, before adding, "If the fates allow." Acknowledging the loss in her life and in the lives of her fans, it's a moment as swift and clear as a teardrop. Closing with, "Don't you all wait, no/Have it now," she seems to have found the simplest way possible to deliver the song from the clutches of nostalgia. This is about the possibility in the moment.

Her minor-keyed take on "My Favorite Things" follows a similarly simple path while getting at the pain in the song. On a decidedly un–hip hop album, this may be the most hip hop moment—if hip hop could be understood as a radical repurposing of one's surroundings. When Blige sings "Cream-colored ponies and crisp apple strudels/Doorbells and sleigh bells and schnitzel with noodles," this doesn't sound like Mary J. Blige's reality, but the absolute conviction in her voice says it is. And it doesn't take a moment's reflection to understand that this is her reality in the same way it is the reality of every child who grew up singing along with *The Sound of Music*. She conjures an almost Dickensian image of a child with her nose pressed to a shop window, the shop itself somewhere in her dreams. The last line is a wistful repetition of the closing words, "so bad," four times. There is no denying the suffering behind the lyric. Instead, there's an argument for all the carols that come after.

# 25

# Think Like a Man Too

Though the sequel to *Think Like a Man* and the second comedy based on Steve Harvey's best-selling 2009 book, *Act Like a Lady, Think Like a Man*, seemed designed for an upwardly mobile young urban professional audience, Blige's role at the helm of the soundtrack said this movie could be about real people, working-class people. Blige told the press she was excited to accept the challenge of a movie soundtrack because of the great history of soundtracks in music history. Of course, *Waiting to Exhale* helped build Blige's career, but soul music history is shaped by Isaac Hayes's *Shaft* (1971), Curtis Mayfield's *Super Fly* (1972), and Diana Ross's *Lady Sings the Blues* (1972), all of which directly ushered in Marvin Gaye's *Trouble Man* (1972), James Brown's *Black Caesar* (1973), and Diana Ross's follow-up, *Mahogany* (1975).

Not surprisingly, then, Blige uses the soundtrack to celebrate those who have inspired her. She opens with a tribute to Jody Watley and Shalamar, covering "A Night to Remember" before explicitly name-checking a list of inspirations on "Vegas Nights"— Michael Jackson, Gladys Knight, Lionel Richie, Marvin Gaye, Otis Redding, Sam Cooke, Aretha Franklin, Roberta Flack, and James Brown. Some of these artists are fellow soundtrack authors, some of them are friends, but they all share the distinction of being among Blige's greatest childhood inspirations.

Though today, audiences don't even expect movies and soundtracks to resemble each other closely, in this case, that's the film's loss. Blige's soundtrack does a better job of getting at the movie's ideas than the film does itself. And that's both what makes this soundtrack a special record and what is certain to limit its appeal to Blige's casual audience. Like the movie, Blige's record is fun and sophisticated, sublimating some of the singer's churchier and funkier qualities to sounds appropriate to a couples' fantasy vacation in Vegas. In that sense, this music steps almost as far outside of the street-Mary persona as the Christmas record does. However, the subject matter here allows her to tackle core themes directly—particularly love, independence, and equality.

Blige enlists throughout what has at this point become her core team—Rodney Jerkins, Tricky Stewart, and The-Dream—and the entirety of the album flows nicely out of the template set by the opening Shalamar cover, with its emphasis on guitar, shining keys, and horns over an effervescent rhythm track. "Vegas Nights" puts a bass guitar up front and focuses on keys, giving the sense that the record's moved deeper into the club.

"Moment of Love" is the dance floor showstopper. Blige repeats, "This is when everybody get on the floor, and then we rock," setting scene and action. The bass throbs through the floor, and keys and horns move like swirling lights. Blige sings "I'm getting my Diana Ross on," paying yet another tribute, this time to the premier moviemaking R&B queen. A nervous-rhythmed search for a missed connection on that floor comes next, the Pharrell Williams–produced "See That Boy Again," repeated false endings suggesting the *Twilight Zone*-like trap the club can become.

On "Wonderful," Blige embraces the happiness that sometimes makes such traps worth the risk. She draws on a young production team—Ronald "Flippa" Colson, Warren "*Oak*" Felder, and Andrew "*Pop*" Wansel from Philly along with Stephen "AceFace" Mostyn from New York—to provide a magical hip hop context. A sample of "the boom, the bip, the boom bip" from A Tribe Called

Quest's "Push It Along" forms a human rhythm bed, and Blige's vocals bounce all over it. The Isley Brothers get name-checked too, as Blige sums up a simple dream, listening to the classic soul band with her lover by her side, her voice soaring over swirling keys.

But then Blige returns to the reality of marriage with "Kiss and Make Up." The heart of this call for reconciliation is the marital warning she repeats in a fast ride of the bass, "This ain't for everybody, this ain't for everybody." The vocal's exalted heights convey both the joy and pain that come out of commitment, staggered beats telegraphing the struggle.

Then, the album explores relationship territory as murky as any Blige has tackled before. "'Cause of you I am better and I'm worse," a weathered Blige sings. This song has all of the album's core elements—insistent beats, prominent bass, horns and keys—but the emphasis is on the heaviest qualities of each sound; even Blige's voice deepens. This is a song about relationship insanity, particularly thinking the same solutions will lead to different results.

On the album's first single, "Suitcase," Blige returns to the theme of self-care, making a break for mental health. Destiny's Child producer Mark J. Feist rains piano notes from the sky, blasts voices from all directions, and pulses synth like the sound of a palpitating heart. This is a song that somehow finds hope in the grim question, "I wonder if I took these scars and pour dirt in 'em, would I grow me a brand new heart?"

And then things get really dark.

"I Want You" builds a battering ram out of every sound that's come before, and it uses this to pound on a door that doesn't want to open. Blige is singing with this new alto again, but this time a scream flickers at the edges. "Can I be honest, can I be honest, yeah?" she asks at her lover's keyhole. Fugees producer Jerry "Wonda" Duplessis does everything imaginable to push Blige's voice, adding a second pulsing horn line on the bridge and mocking echoes in rebuttal to her words. A guitar solo eventually edges this into a Led Zeppelin–like surrealism, and Blige herself mimics Robert Plant in response to the riffing. She's never sounded so naked and unhinged, and the effect is more than a little scary. But that heavy metal excess can also be heard as a distancing mechanism, and when she ends with a wordless Rihanna-like fillip, the reeling chaos comes to rest on a dime.

"Self Love" follows, delivering an ambivalent statement that's part kiss-off, part last chance. Blige collaborates with Darhyl Camper Jr. (producer for John Legend and Mariah Carey) for a delicate soul fabric to manage the nuance of the situation. She's still pounding at the door, and the keyboard effects here threaten rain. Still, this song is every bit the melodic and reflective opposite of "I Want You." There's a rhythm to her beat this time that says she can walk away if she has to, and she has clear demands: "I want you to love me like I'm you." Quietly as funny as it is sad and strong, this song allows Mary J. Blige to embrace the conflicted heart of the blues.

Blige then teams with Tricky Stewart and The-Dream for the album's closing suite, starting with the Blige cowrite "Power Back." A snaky bit of synth pokes its head up over a deliberate strut of a bass line, and a lightly comic show of strength begins to replace the weaknesses that came before. She's found a way to laugh at the situation. Percussion and keys build as she lays out her strategy for moving forward. "Go ahead and lose yourself, I'm going to stay intact," she sings, commenting on the way he gives her more attention when she quits looking for it. Whatever he chooses to do, she has to set her own compass and stick to it. A minor hip hop tour de force about overcoming codependency, the song grows increasingly energetic and triumphant. "All Fun and Games" builds on a similar arrangement, conceding the tragedy underneath the all-too-common carelessness, "and the one that you lost you love the most." Truth is coming to light, and it's announced in bold and bright terms.

"Better" answers in hushed tones, repeating the command "Shh. . . . Be quiet." Blige's deep alto returns to state the facts about Love, an actual character in the song. "Love will tell you about a love that you don't have, and Love will tell you it's good when it's all bad." The song builds into a head-spinning series of contradictions that illustrate confusion, and the distance evident in the song, a kind of Prince-like irony, allows the singer to take comfort in the acceptance of the contradictions.

That acceptance has to happen to make room for "Propose," perhaps the most romantic song Mary J. Blige has ever sung. Fittingly, it's also one of the most beautiful. A simple arrangement, she sings over church piano, clapped percussion, and, eventually, delicately layered synth, chimes, horns, and strings. "Propose" is both a wedding song and an anthem. She sings, "All the imperfections in this world create a perfect us," and offers to get down on bended knee for her lover. Part of what makes the song poignant is that gender reversal, the woman making the proposal, but that's all amplified by the fact that the woman proposing has just told you every conceivable reason why this relationship business shouldn't work. It's the leap of faith that keeps any of us trying at all.

There's something else going on too. It's the fact that, always, since *What's the 411?*, Mary J. Blige has made it clear that her songs of commitment work on a level beyond any single romantic relationship. This is the girl who first told listeners "all my love is all I have" twenty-two years before and pledged that love to an audience that would give her a little respect. Over the course of those years, Blige earned that respect countless times over, creating the concept of a Queen of Hip Hop Soul and redefining it every step to this place she's reached today—the down sister on the project roof, an angel of the ghetto, a maturing woman with a great big ear for a variety of music and the varied audiences that come with it.

As a whole, *Think Like a Man Too* pays tribute to Blige's influences in order to find her place in a chain of tradition. Before she's finished, she's summed up her vision of the necessity of love as a necessity of struggle. A warm palm to the listener's cheek, "Propose" renews her vows.

# 26

# The London Sessions

Blige no doubt knew that a 2014 soundtrack record for a romantic comedy would hardly be noticed outside of her core audience. That core put *Think Like A Man Too* in the *Billboard* Hip Hop/ R&B Top Ten and even placed it at number thirty on the Top Two Hundred albums chart, but opening week was the best week in the lowest-new-sales season Blige had ever seen. With hot young black actresses Taraji P. Henson, Gabrielle Union, and Regina Hall making dollars rain over the heads of actors Michael Ealy, Terrence Jenkins, and a money-grasping Kevin Hart, the album cover certainly didn't make it plain this was a real Mary J. Blige album.

For such reasons, Blige didn't invest much energy promoting her record. Her duet with young Brit singer Sam Smith on "Stay with Me" had been all over the Internet for days, and his debut album came out the same day as the soundtrack. The night of his record release, June 17, 2014, Smith played Harlem's Apollo Theater, and Blige joined him for his encore performance of the hit. The video of that moment went viral, showing an American icon's embrace of the U.K.'s current neo-soul movement. As they ended singing the refrain "stay with me" back and forth to one another and closing with a hug, it felt like a real connection between two improbably shy and sweet kindred spirits.

This was part of a larger campaign by Blige. For some time, her friend Elton John had been encouraging her to do more live recording with a band in the studio. At the same time, inspired by the extraordinary success of first Amy Winehouse and then Adele, Blige heard a way forward for her in what was happening across the water. As she told the *Guardian*'s Tom Horan in August 2014, Blige went to London to record because she was attracted by the U.K.'s emphasis on "proper songs," and she was also drawn by a sense of freedom, adding that "music is free over here the way it used to be in the States." Part of what she'd loved about Winehouse, in fact, had been the singer's ability to reach beyond conventional boundaries. Of Winehouse, Blige told *Billboard* in November 2014, "When I saw her perform, it was scary how amazing she was, all that emotion and that almost Nina Simone–type singing." (While there, Blige made a point of having dinner with Winehouse's father.)

Blige's active interest in performing English pop began when she reached out to the London house music duo Disclosure at the end of 2013, asking if she could cover their song, "F for You." Instead, the duo collaborated with her on a remix, which came out February 5, 2014. The remix single broke the U.K. Top Ten dance chart, made number twenty-two on the U.K. singles chart, and broke the Top Forty on the US dance chart.

By July of 2014, Blige left for London to spend a month making an album at RAK Studios. *The London Sessions* was released in November, debuting on *Billboard*'s Top Ten and at number one on its Hot R&B/Hip-Hop chart. After nearly seven years of declining press attention, Blige received positive reviews for the album in most major media outlets. She also got the cover of *Billboard* and received an extensive review in *Time* magazine. The *New York Times*'s Jon Pareles placed her album in his Top Ten for 2014.

The general consensus was, "Mary's back!" Horan, in that *Guardian* story, talked about a revival of creativity that began when Blige did the "F for You" remix, calling it "the most original thing she'd done in years." *Time*'s Jamieson Cox called that the moment "everything changed." In a December review, *Spin*'s

Brennan Carley wrote, "*The London Sessions* is everything Mary J. Blige has been working towards for what feels like a decade." *Rolling Stone*'s Chuck Arnold called the album "a reboot," suggesting it would restart her career. Andy Kellman, writing for AllMusic, spoke the conventional wisdom, "*The London Sessions* just happens to have her best round of songs, productions, and performances since *The Breakthrough*."

As a fan of Mary J. Blige and the London album, I was happy to see her get all of this positive critical attention. I was also worried about the new mythology, built as it is upon a decided lack of appreciation for almost a decade of her work. *Time*'s Cox got close to the heart of the matter when he asserted, "Her recent projects have seemed explicitly designed to appeal to her base—namely adult black women, the kind who have followed her through personal turmoil and tremendous success since the halcyon days of *What's the 411?* and *My Life*."

While Blige has never neglected that audience (that loyalty being core to her artistic sensibility), such an assessment overlooks the way Blige has consistently burst past genre limitations, laying the groundwork for this British collaboration, most noticeably, at the close of *My Life II*. It doesn't explain the more varied contemporary dance and hip hop features of each of her recent albums, and it doesn't take into account her recurring explorations of harder rock sounds, culminating in the unhinged lunacy of *Think Like a Man Too*'s "I Want You." Cox's assessment does sum up the impression of a popular music press that does not pay much attention to adult black women while it does pay an inordinate amount of attention to what's hip in London.

To my ears, what's new about *The London Sessions* is mostly a matter of younger and different listeners. Although Blige makes smart decisions throughout, what she's doing is not exactly new. Almost everything here is actually musically retro in a way Blige has rarely allowed herself, particularly the decision to play a role she'd always avoided, that of a house music diva, on three of the cuts. (The closest she'd come before was *My Life II*'s cover of Rufus and Chaka Khan's 1983 single "Ain't Nobody"—which is a natural for Blige because it's paying tribute to the funky Chicago sounds that birthed the form.) The risk Blige takes here is leaving the platform that has served her so well and taking hold of hip hop and soul as it swings back to her through European pop. Stepping outside of herself to rediscover herself actually makes this album a piece of a process that started with the Christmas record.

All of that said, there are many reasons to be thankful about this end of that process. Having Blige's longtime collaborator Rodney "Darkchild" Jerkins along certainly helps to bridge the gap between what Blige has done before and what she can do with this new U.K. crew. Together, they hone a focused album that sums up Blige's key themes over the past decade. Pareles summed up much of what makes the record special: "Mary J. Blige's new British collaborators . . . had the brilliantly straightforward idea of exposing her voice, whether it's backed by gospel-y piano or austere house beats." Blige's voice does have a supple touch and warmth that has sometimes been obscured in her American releases, which were often more vividly experimental and certainly more overtly hip hop. *The London Sessions*'s chief strength is its clarity.

Though about half of the cuts feature European house music elements, Blige plays the disco diva on only three of them—"My Loving," "Nobody But You," and "Follow." Neither technically or aesthetically built for the bombastic wailing over mechanistic beats typical of the form, Blige never wanted to do this work (and might not have technically managed it) when she was younger. However, at this point in her career, she makes the most of the extreme dynamics of the genre—turning the punching bag rhythms into hard emotional workouts and grabbing ethereal keyboard washes for reflection. The album opener talks about therapy the singer does "two times a day," and these dance cuts show music serving that purpose. Each offering the brag the dance floor wants, "My Loving" luxuriates in the singer's sexuality, "Nobody But You" celebrates a focused desire, and "Follow" defines the singer's aesthetic credo—"Give it love or give it up." All take place in a troubled relationship. Hence, the need for the punching bag.

The workout analogy is important because this is an album

about "doing the work." The opener, "Therapy," uses a stark gospel arrangement—choir, tambourine, organ, bass, and drums—for what feels like Blige's answer to Amy Winehouse's biggest hit, "Rehab" (an old-school-R&B-styled rejection of getting clean). "Therapy" is a confession that nothing has been fixed—the singer is "unhappy," "alone," "bitter," self-loathing, suffering from insomnia, stressed, and driven, and it's all taking a toll on the relationship she clings to for sanity—but over and over in any given day, she does what she has to in order to gain perspective.

"Doubt" uses the sounds of "The Living Proof"—a simple, southern piano figure and sweeping strings—as a less grandiose, more portable reminder of all the reasons she has to believe she can make it one more day. Against acoustic guitar also reminiscent of the close of *My Life II*, "When You're Gone" serves as a reminder why the singer wants her marriage to make it one more day too.

Not that the album doesn't throw down a few gauntlets. The most Disclosure-flavored track here—all washes of sound and blasts of keyboard over techno beats—is a relationship climax. Nodding to Dead or Alive's 1985 dance floor hit "You Spin Me Round (Like a Record)" (and no doubt Flo Rida's 2009 use of the sample), she declares, "I'm turning it right round," before declaring, "My love won't be the same for you no more." This is the end of something but, tellingly, not the relationship as a whole.

Clearly the album's climax is "Whole Damn Year," one of two collaborations with Emeli Sandé. It's a tough meditation over the gentlest piano arpeggios and hard, staggered beats. The song's narrative explains why "you can't touch me tonight." And though it's a song about healing, part of the process is a recitation of the violence—"Spring punched me right in the stomach/Summer came looking for blood." It's a shattering series of moments, each step thoughtful, precise, and beautiful. In a refrain that declares, "It's been a bad five years," Blige's voice gives that final word a quaver that communicates both deep pain and a supple kind of strength. She's never sounded better.

Carrying forward a core of her tradition, the other most powerful moments on this album are a series of confrontations with a lover. Over chorded piano and a gradual drum build, Blige delivers the message "There's only so much I can do if you're not loving you" with both tender sorrow and gospel intensity. By contrast, "Long Hard Look" uses retro synth, big drums, and bass to declare authoritatively that this relationship could work if her lover would simply "look at yourself" and "look at us now." The album closes with "Worth My Time," defining the need for respect. All voice over chorded piano (a slight aura of strings sneaks in at the bridge), Blige promises, "I won't give up," but the bottom line is "it isn't enough to get by." Declaring, "I want to stay," Blige hangs onto the album's last syllable, rippling that "y" like smoke from a guttering flame.

# 27

# Being with You

"Love is an action word," Mary J. Blige sang toward the end of her performance of "My Life" on 2004's *Live from Los Angeles*.

She followed that statement as she had to—"I gotta keep moving." She repeated the line like a mantra, offering both an explanation of how she had always worked and a pledge to continue to do so for her fans.

Then she called, "Keep on moving, you all," repeating it several times before pleading, "Don't let 'em stop you!"

It has been her modus operandi from the beginning, a beginning that started with a description of love and a search for love. Sean Combs knew her well, wanting to name her the "Queen of Ghetto Love." Andre Harrell's revision of the title to "Queen of Hip Hop Soul" was simply a way to connect the concept to the cultural influences that gave shape to Blige and reinforced the theme— the genres that stood for black love and spiritual regeneration. The Beatles may have sung "All You Need Is Love," but the hard work of loving has been most consistently explored in smaller statements, the bread and butter of popular music, love songs— nowhere more thoroughly than in the overlapping "adult" genres of country music and soul music. Regardless of genre, women have been the clearest voices sussing through how that love might work, and Mary J. Blige has been exceptional among those women.

From the start, Blige built concept albums around the mystery and necessity of love. She broadened her interpretation of hip hop and soul to include everything from the heaviest rock to the gentlest voice over piano, always reaching for the voices of women all but forgotten in the mainstream culture. She allowed her efforts to understand love to move her from a focus on surviving the blues to a vision of a community liberated by new levels of honesty and commitment.

A decade into her career, Blige explicitly pursued a spirituality as inclusive as her music. Her spiritual stance was consistent with feminist theorist bell hooks's description of the concept in her 2001 book, *All about Love*. Hooks wrote, "Spiritual life is first and foremost about commitment to a way of thinking and behaving that honors principles of inter-being and interconnectedness." When Blige has talked about self-care and her own pursuits of spiritual refinement, she has done so as a part of a dialogue with her audience.

The search for self-love is a part of her commitment to that audience. She has shown that commitment in various ways. Although always an artist who worked for charitable organizations, Blige's benefit work and public outreach increased in her career's second decade as she began to see the search for love in terms of a search for social justice. She began to talk much more explicitly about class, race, and gender as she expressed compassion for those on different sides of abusive situations.

Blige's search for love has demanded that she deal with messy realities; it has not allowed her the luxury of looking away. This code is perhaps nowhere better illustrated than in her second decade of music, largely focused on what love has to teach us in a committed relationship—about the value of honesty, the balance of independence and interdependence, and the need to fight forward through brokenness, disappointment, and loss. All of this detail work has led her beyond the story of any single relationship, and it has allowed her endless points of connection with her audience.

Mary J. Blige plays a distinctly important role in a unique history of cultural expression. As musicologist Christopher Small argued in his 1987 book *Music of the Common Tongue: Survival and Celebration in African American Music*, "Black people in the Americas and elsewhere have been during the present century at the heart of an outburst of creative energy surely unparalleled in the known history of the human race." Small calls that outburst of energy "musicking," an Afro-American tradition (though not exclusive to black music so much as exemplified by it) that sees music as a transformative participatory activity. The redemptive promise of that activity has been the heart of hip hop and soul, and Small's words force Blige's significance onto the world stage. Mary J. Blige has taken good care of that heart, casting "love is an action word" as a statement of responsibility.

In 1994, Mary J. Blige expressed commitment to a troubled relationship on *My Life*'s "Be with You." In 2006, she delivered "Be without You," an anthem to keeping love alive. In 2014, Smokey Robinson released a duet with Blige, a new version of his number one R&B single, 1981's "Being with You."

The new version of "Being with You" belongs in Blige's canon. The great Motown voice and the voice of hip hop soul trade wordless vocal riffs over plucked guitar chords and an opening drum beat. Blige begins the vocal, singing a pledge she owns, "I don't care what they think. If you're leaving, I'm going to beg you to stay." Robinson immediately chimes in, supporting her through the refrain.

The song moves through stages. At first, it's simply two singers insisting on their dedication to one another despite the push and pull of their relationship and the outside forces that intensify the struggle. Blige's voice finds a high harmony counterpointing Robinson's original melody and deepening the song's texture.

Then Blige's voice aches as she questions her judgment, like the logic that she's in denial takes a bite out of her. But what matters most is the response to this line of questioning. The two voices come together again, defining what makes this interaction unique.

That newfound clarity regarding the sanctity of the relationship changes the song's tone altogether.

Blige's voice soars from this climax to the end. She rejects the criticism and recommits to the struggle. She's testifying on high, while he's urging her on more quietly, with warm assurances in her ear. By the end, they've found enough security with one another that they are able to play. She teases, "Don't you wanna be with me, yeah, yeah, yeah?" He answers, "Wichoo, Mary."

From Motown to Uptown, from rock and roll through hip hop, this feels like a four-minute definition of the heart of soul itself. While the music's lyrics have often been focused upon a specific romantic relationship, the story has always been bigger. Aretha Franklin may have been asking her man for "Respect" and telling him to "Think," but she was speaking for classes of people being ignored by those in power. Similarly, Motown opened the doors to the American dream, and Mary J. Blige's career has been about the needs of those who never got through those doors or who have been shut out of a collapsing system. In that sense, it's even about what a forty-three-year-old woman and a seventy-four-year-old man have to say in an art form they each have fought to mature.

"I don't care about anything else but being with you," Blige sings, and in the context of her career that means she cares about a great deal. It means she cares about maintaining her hip hop roots, and she cares about building and maintaining a connection to a larger tradition of musicking for a more compassionate, inclusive America. It means she cares about being with the victims of 9/11, but it also means she cares about the victims of Katrina and the victims of ongoing human rights struggles in Haiti. It means she cares about the troops and the victims of the troops' actions. It means she cares about people as people.

And it means she cares about the work involved. She cares enough to be the strongest singer she's ever been, twenty-two years into her career. She also cares about constancy and honesty and the spiritual growth that comes with taking care of each other's needs.

If "love is an action word," "being with you" is a calling. Few have honored their vocation with more dedication than Mary J. Blige. Even fewer have made such a convincing argument for the enduring promise of American popular music.

---

In 2008, Black Entertainment Television launched the new awards ceremony BET Honors for broadcast during Black History Month. Mary J. Blige received the award for excellence in entertainment in 2009. On January 24, 2015, Blige returned to that stage to close a ceremony that had honored Usher, Kanye West, Phylicia Rashād, the Smithsonian's Dr. Johnnetta Betsch Cole, and Microsoft chairman John W. Thompson.

She took the stage in a sparkling black evening gown, laughing a little as if nervous about her role. She smiled and looked out at the front rows, stating, "Congratulations to all the amazing honorees tonight. Because you did not give up in the face of adversity, you inspired me to do the same. We celebrate you, we honor you, and we thank you so much for your courage. I want to dedicate this song to all of you."

The piano introduction to her new single "Doubt" began to play, and, in the front row, Mr. West began to rock his head back and forth with the rhythm. Starting with Harriet Tubman, a slide-show of great African Americans (including the honorees) filled a screen above and behind her—Shirley Chisholm, Maya Angelou, Angela Davis, Venus and Serena Williams, and Muhammad Ali, to name a few.

She took the mic out of its stand and walked toward the edge of the stage to sing, "Now you're looking at a leader, now you're looking at a queen." Monitors picked up Dr. Cole's bright look as Blige owned her role. When the singer reached her first triumphant cry, "I can't keep doubting myself anymore," West was grinning wide, and Rashād wore a beatific smile.

But Blige was just getting down to business. Her face now racked with pain, she declared, "You think you know, but you don't know the half." It felt like what it was, a direct conversation that both spoke to and for the audience. Though this event took place a week before the Grammys, the television audience saw West after those other awards, wearing a new controversy over his protest of Beck's album win. Rashād had recently struggled through an ugly media blunder, attempting to defend her longtime costar Bill Cosby from rape allegations and making it sound like she wasn't concerned about the alleged victims. The BET honorees had battle scars, and Blige stood for them all.

As she sang the last refrain, her voice soared. Then she snapped her fingers and repeated, "No, no, no, no, I can't keep doubting myself, no, no, no, no." The audience shot to their feet and roared approval, clapping hard to let her know—even if she wanted to— she couldn't shake their faith in that heart and that voice.

# Selected Discography

Beyond her thirteen full albums of new material, Mary J. Blige released a live album, a best-of collection with new material, two remix albums, and two significantly revised versions of two more albums. She also released two live DVDs, and two behind-the-scenes DVDs. Including twelve-inch vinyl remixes and duets with other artists, Blige plays a featured role in over a hundred other single and EP releases. Choosing the twenty most significant "discs" was not easy, setting aside, as it must, distinctive and important work with (among others) the Notorious B.I.G., Heavy D, Nas, Talib Kweli, Chaka Khan, George Michael, Elton John, Patti LaBelle, Musiq Soulchild, T.I., and her recent career-turning singles with Disclosure and Sam Smith. What made this list, then, were the results of hard choices based on both cultural and artistic concerns. All of the albums are here (in one form or another) because I do think Blige is distinctly important as a consistent and thoughtful album artist, a distinct rarity both in her genre and in our time.

*What's the 411?*, Mary J. Blige (Uptown, 1992). It's startling how much of the story is here, a sensibility already so well formed, with singing material provided by Combs and his team of new jack songwriters. Because the production is so tied to the keyboard effects of its day, this is the only album here that sounds particularly dated, but it still works. That fully present, always reaching voice carves the broad outlines for the story that follows. Half of the ten full songs here were hit singles; all of them might have been.

*My Life*, Mary J. Blige (MCA, 1994). On her first album as a songwriter, Blige cites Marvin Gaye as an inspiration, and the result is an album that makes a remarkable leap in maturity and ambition from the apparent goals of *What's the 411?* Like Gaye's *What's Going On*, *My Life* is an album as a continuous suite of reflections with lush, layered production.

"I'll Be There for You/You're All I Need to Get By," Method Man featuring Mary J. Blige (Def Jam, 1995). Crafted by key members (RZA and Method Man) of the Wu-Tang Clan, the most innovative and authoritative hip hop crew of that moment (perhaps ever), this duet enshrines Blige's place at the heart of the larger rap story. Appropriately enough, her vocals draw on Marvin Gaye and Tammi Terrell.

*Share My World*, Mary J. Blige (MCA, 1997). If *My Life* plumbs greater depths than Blige's debut, this third studio album travels more ground. The Marvin Gaye influence is still here, but the more dramatic shifts in popular music styles call to mind Stevie Wonder on *Songs in the Key of Life*. Serving as it did as a statement of independence from former producer Combs, her first album to debut at number one on *Billboard* reached that top spot as a matter of timing and design.

*The Tour*, Mary J. Blige (MCA, 1998). As funky and hip hop as they are soulful, these twenty-four performances show just how a young Blige grounds the softest textures of *Share My World* in street and gospel grit. Particularly noteworthy for ending with

reverent and moving covers of Aretha Franklin's "Day Dreaming"
and Dorothy Moore's "Misty Blue."

*Mary*, Mary J. Blige (MCA, 1999). Outside of the hip hop press,
this was Blige's first widespread critical favorite. It's a sober, adult
album, the whole first half a jazzy exploration of spirituality. The
far more narrative second half focuses on questions of neglect,
betrayal, independence, and solidarity, every moment key to her
story. Guest appearances by Elton John, Eric Clapton, and Aretha
Franklin declare Blige's significance to the larger pop music story.

*No More Drama*, Mary J. Blige (MCA, 2002). This album originally
came out in 2001, but the 2002 revamp is slightly better. In either
version, this is the first Blige album that might be accused of having some fat over the course of its seventeen songs. That said, it also
has some of the highest highs, including the ridiculously infectious
"Family Affair" and the title track, a declaration so strong it would
affect every move she made hereafter.

"Whenever I Say Your Name," Sting and Mary J. Blige (A&M,
2003). This gorgeous single earned its Grammy for best duet. An
ethereal, serpentine structure allows the two voices to caress each
other in endlessly surprising variations before a funky break gives
Blige the chance to push for gospel intensity. If anything, this five-
and-a-half-minute track ends too soon.

*Love & Life*, Mary J. Blige (Geffen, 2003). Life after "Drama" starts
a little rough, with a technically brilliant album heavy on the spiritual renewal and low in the everyday conflict that ties Blige to her
audience. Ironically, some degree of conflict behind the scenes
may have kept the music more guarded than usual, Blige reuniting
with Combs for this one record before calling off the relationship
once again.

*The Breakthrough*, Mary J. Blige (Geffen/Matriarch, 2005). The title
says it well. Blige finds a way to salt the songs of happiness and

praise with tangible and familiar conflict. Hook-laden, energetic, and richly textured, it's no surprise that this album generated five hit singles. No wasted moments here.

"Runaway Love," Ludacris featuring Mary J. Blige (DTP/Def Jam, 2006). Not many songs get to number two on the pop charts explicitly confronting the reasons young women run away from home. Ludacris's storytelling is crucial, but Blige's riffing on the title offers all the warmth of an extended hand, empathizing with a swirl of conflicting emotions right up to her final call—"Don't keep running away/I'll run away with you if you want me to."

*Reflections (A Retrospective)*, Mary J. Blige (Geffen, 2006). Eight of her previous single releases and a remix of "My Life" don't come close to doing what a "best-of" collection should do, but this does contain her wonderful 2000 duet with Wyclef Jean, "911," as well as four new songs, hallmarked by the catchy and evocative "We Ride (I See the Future)" and the dreamy duet with John Legend, "King & Queen."

*Growing Pains*, Mary J. Blige (Geffen, 2007). As anyone in her sixth year of marriage or third decade of life might understand, the dark corners of *The Breakthrough* have only grown longer and more menacing, so Blige uses bold hip hop beats and samples (and the street-savvy grit of her vocals) to fight her way forward. A great record with, surprisingly, Blige's most ecstatic single, "Just Fine."

"Sumthin's Gotta Give," Big Boi featuring Mary J. Blige (2008). Inspired by Obama's run for presidency, this sweeping portrait of the recession tackles the corrosive effects of trying to stretch a dollar. Blige sings a chorus of nationwide and global vision before taking on the last verse—a portrait of a single mother with a sick child and the soul-crushing guilt of a father on parole.

"Stronger," Mary J. Blige (Interscope, 2009). Originally released on the *More than a Game* soundtrack, this single would eventually be placed on an international revamp of *Stronger with Each Tear* (along with covers of "Stairway to Heaven" and "Whole Lotta Love" that are interesting—especially for the way Blige demystifies the "Stairway" lyric—but not quite worthy of this list). This song, though, soars like the best Rihanna anthems (attributable to both cowriting by Ester Dean and production by Polow da Don), with a depth of experience behind the vocal that's all Blige.

*Stronger with Each Tear*, Mary J. Blige (Geffen, 2009). A woefully underrated album remarkably focused on the importance of getting to know and take care of one's self. Musically, Blige's voice sounds stronger than ever, and the lush arrangements are stunning. Though filled with infectious hooks and featuring duets with youngsters like Drake and Trey Songz, this is certainly the work of a mature woman less concerned than ever with the pop music of the moment.

*My Life II . . . The Journey Continues (Act 1)*, Mary J. Blige (Geffen, 2011). As its title suggests, this album aims high (the sequel to her fans' most cherished album), and work with Nas, Drake, Busta Rhymes, and Beyoncé—not to ignore *The Breakthrough* alter ego Brook Lynn—shows a serious effort to intentionally engage with hip hop and pop's main currents on the scale of 2005's great hit album. None of her records starts with the high energy of the first five cuts here, and no record since *Mary* has had as strong a second half. Though this powerful collection lay the groundwork for most of what's celebrated on *The London Sessions*, it's sadly Blige's most neglected work before the soundtrack album.

*A Mary Christmas*, Mary J. Blige (Verve, 2013). A stunning break from Blige's canon because the hip hop and soul sensibilities that define her voice get used minimally in favor of a traditional pop aesthetic (far more Nat King Cole than Mariah Carey). Her continuously evolving strengths as a singer allow her to make the subtlety work, the gifts of the approach appearing most clearly when the listener stops looking for them.

*Think Like a Man Too*, Mary J. Blige (Epic, 2014). The artist continuously pays tribute to her influences (including soul soundtrack pioneers Marvin Gaye, James Brown, and Diana Ross), marshalling forces to deal with the perils of a disastrous romantic weekend like the one in the movie. The result is both some of Blige's most varied and engaging ear candy ever ("Wonderful" and "Propose") and a comic pit that doesn't stop dropping until it reaches hellfire (the three-song movement from "Cargo" to "I Want You").

*The London Sessions*, Mary J. Blige (Capitol/Matriarch, 2014). This is the first Blige album that might be called retronuevo (or roots R&B). Of course, the roots here pass through a Brit pop filter equally enamored with parlor song simplicity and eighties and nineties house music. Not ignoring some of her most moving and technically proficient vocals, what really makes this work is a strong focus on Blige's key themes regarding the hard-earned struggle of love.

# Acknowledgments

This book wouldn't exist without the following people:

David Cantwell, who recommended me for this series and gave me advice at various points along the way;

Mary Robinson (my mom), who filled my childhood with Diana Ross, Gladys Knight, and Aretha Franklin;

James McGraw, my older brother, who introduced me to everyone from Joan Armatrading to Patti Smith;

Dave Marsh, who invited me into music journalism while warning me against it; his work is a bone-deep influence here; I'm also very thankful for his early advice on my draft;

Lee Ballinger, who wrote a piece about Joyce Sims in 1986 that changed the way I heard women in R&B and dance music; his writing about MJB is a specific influence here;

William "Billy Chin" Heaster, who, in 1987, handed me a TDK SA90 that took my naïve interest in hip hop, soul, and funk into depths I've never wanted to escape;

Bernice Alverson, my coworker at the start of my hip hop journey, who schooled me daily on hearing outside of my race and gender;

Sarah Funck, my oldest daughter, who was born the year MJB debuted and who guided me through a musical second childhood;

Trionna Alexander, my younger daughter, who schools me about music (and just about everything else) every day;

C. J. Janovy, who began plotting a book about women and music with me two decades ago and who gave me very helpful advice on this manuscript.

And it would be a much lesser book without help from the following people:

Melissa Blazek, who championed this idea every step of the way, brainstorming ideas and offering her considerable resources;

Stratlist and Dadooronron, two music email lists filled with friends I consult on a regular basis, including Lauren Onkey, Charles Hughes, Eric Schumacher-Rasmussen, Stewart Francke, John Floyd, Steven J. Messick, Cheryl Burns, and Alexander Shasko;

Marie Ramos, who was a great adviser on my research trip to Georgia;

Kevin Alexander Gray and Park Bucker, who gave me a home base in South Carolina and who taught me more about the South than I could have thought to ask;

Craig Werner and Daniel Wolff, both there for a long list of questions, helped me with the rough outlines of gospel and gave me advice on my early drafts, Craig commenting on virtually every page of the first full draft.

Others who were always there with their advice, support, and encouragement include Jennifer Clarkson, Sam Bell, Brooke Heagerty, Rachel Kimbrough, Luke Sheafer, Jane Blakeley, Mike Warren, and my father, Roger Alexander.

And then there were the interviewees. Kansas City singer Darcus Gates opened her doors to me so I could talk with Alyson Williams, and in the process, I also met Glenn Jones, his thoughts on the ongoing tensions between gospel and mainstream R&B enormously helpful. Jeff Redd, Chucky Thompson, Miki Howard, Dorothy Moore, and Channette and Channoah Higgens were all kind, patient, and generous with their thoughts. A special thanks to the beautiful people of Richmond Hill, Georgia, for the hospitality and the history.

And then there was Karyn White, who gave me the idea of including the variety of fan testimonials I encountered whenever I told people what I was doing. Danyel Smith's beautiful *Essence* essay "Why Mary Matters" played a role too. Thank you to Ann Cox, Natasha Ria El-Scari, Jay Harris, Toni Hill, Itzel Lopez, and Mia Styles for putting in words the way so many others feel. While I was writing, Treva B. Lindsey, Regina N. Bradley, Tanisha C. Ford, and Emily J. Lordi did some amazing work (including a 2014 YouTube dialogue on *My Life*) that affirmed and inspired what I was doing throughout the finishing stages.

Of course, I owe a great deal to my editor, Casey Kittrell, and his assistant, Angelica Lopez, at the University of Texas Press, as well as series editor David Menconi and copy editors Molly Frisinger and Abby Webber. With great thoughtfulness, they pushed me to take another look, and another, at the details that could make a world of difference.

Extra special thanks go to my greatest soundboard and supporter, Lauren Ingraham. Her love of MJB no doubt helped her deal with my past two years' obsessiveness. Somehow, she's still here and still helping. When she reads these words, she may just believe my many claims that it's finished.

It feels clichéd but it's true—everyone above deserves credit for what I got right; what I got wrong, including every unlisted friend who played a role, that's all on me.